CROCHET
PATTERNS
FOR BEGINNERS

A complete guide to start and have fun with easy stitches and projects.

Sarah Boulard

© **Copyright 2020 by Sarah Boulard - All rights reserved.**

The content contained within this book may not be reproduced, duplicated or transmitted without direct written permission from the author or the publisher.

Under no circumstances will any blame or legal responsibility be held against the publisher, or author, for any damages, reparation, or monetary loss due to the information contained within this book. Either directly or indirectly.

Legal Notice:

This book is copyright protected. This book is only for personal use. You cannot amend, distribute, sell, use, quote or paraphrase any part, or the content within this book, without the consent of the author or publisher.

Disclaimer Notice:

Please note the information contained within this document is for educational and entertainment purposes only. All effort has been executed to present accurate, up to date, and reliable, complete information. No warranties of any kind are declared or implied. Readers acknowledge that the author is not engaging in the rendering of legal, financial, medical or professional advice. The content within this book has been derived from various sources. Please consult a licensed professional before attempting any techniques outlined in this book.

By reading this document, the reader agrees that under no circumstances is the author responsible for any losses, direct or indirect, which are incurred as a result of the use of information contained within this document, including, but not limited to, — errors, omissions, or inaccuracies.

Table of Contents

Introduction 4

Chapter 1   Understand Crochet and Patterns 8

Chapter 2   Tools and Materials 24

Chapter 3   How to Crochet 35

Chapter 4   Patterns 51

Chapter 5   Types Of Crochet 67

Chapter 6   Types Of Projects 74

Chapter 7   Mistakes and Solutions 82

Chapter 8   Tips And Tricks To Crocheting 89

Chapter 9   Crochet Goal 95

Chapter 10   Holding the Yarn 101

Conclusion 107

Introduction

There isn't an exact date when crochet started. It has been mentioned throughout earlier times. Experts claim that this craft has been around as early as 1500 to 1800 BC. Basing on the hand technique of basic crochet, it is presumed to have originated in the Middle East. Some claim that crochet originated in China and only spread to its neighboring countries such as the Middle East and eventually to Europe.

Crochet became most notable when French nuns started to crate elaborate and delicate patterns. They were known to create complex lacework using very fine materials. They made table clothes used to cover the altar and adorn the church. It was said that the art of crochet was a closely guarded craft among the nuns. It became an integral part of life in the convent.

Over the next years, crochet found its way to Scotland and England. From the nuns, the knowledge and skill were passed on to the upper class. Crochet circles were established among the ladies of the upper class. The work was no longer focused on delicate and complex lace but was just as elegant. During those times, the skill was limited among the upper class. The poor were not given the privilege to learn the craft.

During the Renaissance, both the upper and lower classes were practicing crochet. During this time, the ladies were using macramé, which is several fine threads knotted together. They made delicate lacework which became popular across Europe.

In the 1820s, crochet was introduced in Ireland. They used fine threads and made delicate work that imitated English lace. It became known as Irish lace. Over the next years, Irish lace became very popular in Europe, especially in the Balkans.

By the early 1900s, yarns changed from fine threadlike materials to something much thicker. Hook sizes also changed in order to accommodate the thicker yarns. Patterns started even more simplified, a deviation from the complex lacework in previous years. Crochet items progressed from lacework such as table covers and church adornments, into something more practical such as gloves and scarves.

Today, crochet skills are too simple compared to how the French nuns used to make them. The craft has become widespread, but the skill levels can be compared to the level of primary school crochet. It is still considered fabulous but way below the level that crochet used to be.

Also, compared to decades ago, there are considerably fewer people who are interested in the craft. Learning the skill is no longer confined to closed groups, but fewer people are willing to try. Mass production and cheaper goods have made people less inclined to making their own socks or blankets.

However, there are still a considerable number of people who keep the skill ever evolving. There are still people who wish to learn the craft.

Today's patterns are simpler. Popular ones include baby items such as sweaters, socks, bonnets, booties and blankets. Other items include Afghans and adult wear such as scarves, socks and sweaters.

Clothing can be made through many means, and one of which is crochet. Some of the other methods include weaving, bonding, and the one that is closely related to crochet, knitting, etc. Crochet has, however, evolved from the process of making just clothing to making other decorative stuff.

Crotchet is definitely an enjoyable way out of boredom. There is no need to be idle anymore as you can make something beautiful during your free moments. You can take a leave from work, and while you enjoy your favorite movies on Zeeworld, hold a hook, yarn in your hands, and make a cozy blanket.

If you certainly acknowledge how to crochet, you will find an incredible variety of exceptional and charming, extraordinary worth guides to give it a shot.

Crochet guides you through the basic frameworks and secures giving information about photographs and pictures that can be used as first patterns. The little projects fuse things going from a direct chain line wrist knickknack to an in the current style intarsia pad.

At the point when you are confident with all the crochet secures, you can dispatch into the projects part and begin making crocheted things as different as a traditional granny spread for a newborn child, an unobtrusive flower pincushion, and a youngster's midyear tunic dress.

Crochet will engage you to make your own excellent, uncommonly made crocheted pieces for yourself, your home, additionally, your friends and family.

When making things, for instance, garments, or various projects for which measure is critical, it is continually fitting to crochet a check swatch first in the yarn you hope to use; if your check swatch is smaller than that recommended, you may need to use a greater catch; in case it is greater, use a smaller catch. With various projects, the check is authentically not a basic segment, for example, the liners, and the catlike bushel, ought not to be an unequivocal size.

As you become continuously experienced as a crocheted, so you will get acquainted with which catch sizes are appropriate for the different sorts of yarn.

Never use secures on a toy that is for a newborn child or particularly little adolescent, since there is the danger that the child could smother or ingest it, easily removable parts on toys must be isolated. If you are using prosperity eyes on toys, reliably guarantee that they are in line with current security rules.

Despite an extensive manual for basic join and methods, crochet gives an expansive presentation of line surfaces, crocheted edgings, openwork, and color work, similarly as a manual for making granny squares and stunning flowers, all with structures. Use these to develop your basic crocheting aptitudes, before setting out on progressively daring and astounding crochet models, and you will find yourself arranged to make any project you want.

Chapter 1   Understand Crochet and Patterns

One of the most intimidating parts about learning to crochet is reading the pattern. At first glance, it may seem rather complicated, but as you become familiar with crochet knowledge, you'll soon see that it is not all that bad.

The first thing you need to do before you know how to read a crochet pattern is to check the abbreviations used for all of the various stitches. You will use these symbols repeatedly when reading a pattern and you'll learn most of them easily. The table below includes a list of the most commonly used stitches and their abbreviations.

These abbreviations are essential for hook-craft as they are meant to make patterns easier for you by following all the standards for the methodology of crocheting. Therefore, you must know all these abbreviations; else, the crocheting experience will become awfully confusing for you. And the best part, these abbreviations are simple to understand that you will learn them in no time at all.

ABBR.	DEFINITION	EXPLANATION
beg	begin/beginning	*This is an indication of where to start stitching. It is usually the first part of the instructions and will be after the chain stitch*
bpdc	back post double crochet	*The double crochet will be done on the vertical post of the next stitch. Enter the hook from the back, so the stitch is formed behind the previous row.*

bpsc	back post single crochet	*The single crochet will be done on the vertical post of the next stitch. Enter the hook from the back, so the stitch is formed behind the previous row.*
bptr	back post triple crochet	*The triple crochet will be done on the vertical post of the next stitch. Enter the hook from the back, so the stitch is performed on behind the previous row*
CC	Contrast color	*When working with more than one color yarn, this is an indicator to use the contrasting color*
ch-	(ch-#)	*Chain stitch for the number indicated. Many times, the ch-# is often an instruction at the end of a row because it creates a stitch to begin a subsequent row and allows sufficient space to turn to the other side of the work.*
ch sp	chain space	*A chain space is created by skipping over stitches in the previous row and using chain stitch instead.*
cl	cluster stitch	*Also called the shell stitch. It is a series of stitches that form a diamond shape that looks like a shell.*

dc	double crochet	*Insert hook, front to back, bring your yarn from the ball of yarn towards you while draping it onto the hook; bring the hook back to the front of the project with the new loop of yarn. Drape the yarn again and work the hook through 2 of the loops on the hook. Repeat so that you can pull yarn through the remaining two loops. You will have one loop remaining on the hook.*
dec	decrease	*Make the row shorter by combining stitches. This alters the shape of the textile.*
inc	increase/increases/increasing	*Increase the number of stitches in a row or round by adding one or more additional stitches.*
lp(s)	loops(s)	*The drawing yarn upon your crochet hooks to be used to create a stitch or advance your stitches.*
oz	ounce(s)	*The weight of the yarn you will use in crochet is usually measured in ounces. The weight of the yarn matters in determining if it is appropriate for the*

		project and how much will be needed to complete it.
pc	popcorn stitch	*Stitch that creates a raised surface in your crochet. It is created by making a number of double or triple crochet in on stitch from the row below and finishing in a point at the top of the stitch.*
rem	remaining	*The number of stitches left in a row or round.*
rep	repeat	*Command to do a stitch or set of stitches over again for the prescribed number of times.*
rnd(s)	round(s)	*Rounds are rows, but for circular patterns. Sometimes it's hard to determine where the round ends. This is where stitch markers come in handy.*
RS	right side	*Considered the visible side of a crochet pattern. Most crochet looks the same way for both front and back. Others have one side the is considered the front.*
sc	single crochet	*The basic stitch. Put your hook through*

		a stitch in the previous row, wrap the yarn from the ball loosely around the hook, and bring the new loop so that it passes through both of them on the crochet hook.
sk	skip	Avoid stitching in the next stitch, or number of stitches indicated in the pattern
sl st	slip stitch	Created by inserting a crochet hook through a stitch or space, whatever the pattern says, and grabbing the yarn from the ball and wrapping it loosely around the hook. Bring the new loop back, so that is the only loop left on the hook.
sp(s)	space(s)	Space is a hole or space created with crochet stitches. It generally is a direction to make a stitch in the space created by the previous stitch pattern.
st(s)	stitch(es)	A singular or multiple series of loops pulled through other stitches and interwoven into a pattern using a crochet hook.

tog	together	*Perform a series of stitches together in the same space to create one extended stitch*
tr	triple crochet	*Insert hook, yarn over twice, bring one loop back through, and there will be four loops on the hook. Wrap the yarn from the ball loosely around the hook and bring it through two loops, repeating until there is only one loop left.*
WS	wrong side	*Most crochet looks the same way for both front and back. If there is a pattern being formed on only one side of the fabric, the wrong side is the side of the piece where the pattern is not present.*
yd(s)	yard(s)	*Yarn comes in yards. The number of yards necessary to complete a project is sometimes listed on in the pattern instructions.*
yo	yarn over	*An instruction to place the yarn over the hook so that I may be brought back through the stitches or through a loop or loops on the crochet hook.*

Symbols

When you are looking at crochet patterns, you will often see that along with the abbreviations, there are symbols. The symbols are there to instruct you on how to complete a group of stitches.

( ) *Parentheses* have information inside which groups more than one crochet stitch that needs to be completed at one time.

For example, there may be a simple sequence to be performed like (sl st, 2 hdc, sc) in next ch-4 sp.

These instructions mean to do a slipstitch in the space created with a chain 4 command in the previous row. Then do two half double crochets and single crochet in the same space. All the stitches will be in one single crochet space. You may also see the parentheses providing additional information regarding the row or round in which you are working.

These are often shown in italics; *(54, sl st, ch 3, sl st)* indicates that there should be 54 of the series, slip stitch, chain 3, slip stitch. It is simply telling you how many there should be in the row. The parenthesis break up the various directions and groups them together so you can tell what needs to be done in a specific row or round.

[ ] *Brackets* are an indication of something that will be repeated. The number of times to repeat will be outside of the brackets.

It will say, for example, [sc, dc, sc in ch-1 sp] 12 times.

This will mean to do the series, sc-dc-sc in a chain-one space in the row for twelve chain-one spaces. A series of stitches form a pattern that will add variety to any project. There may also be items bold and in brackets that indicate a different number of rows or stitches due to variations of size.

This looks like Rounds 14-15 [16-17, 16-18]. The numbers in the brackets signify the rounds that will be affected for the large sizes when the pattern is for more than one size.

{ } Between the *braces*, you will find instructions that will be repeated in the same way as brackets. These will sometimes be used inside of parentheses or brackets if there is a repeated action within a repeated action. The braces isolate a particular action to be repeated. [hdc in next sc, ch-4, skip dc, {sc in next 11 ch}] 14 times. This is moving into territory beyond beginners.

* The most common symbol you will probably see in patterns is the asterisk. The asterisk is used to indicate the start of a sequence. Typically, it will be followed by instructions to do the sequence from the start and how many times to repeat it. Take a look at this sequence *sc in next dc, dc in next ch-4 space, hdc next12 dc, rep from * to end of the row, ending with dc.

Something to keep in mind is that crochet terms differ in the UK and the US. This table will help you should you ever need this information.

Crochet Terms Used in UK and US

British Notation	American Notation
double crochet (dc)	single crochet (sc)
half treble (htr)	half double crochet (hdc)
treble (tr)	double crochet (dc)
double treble (dtr)	treble (tr)
triple treble (trtr)	double treble (dtr)
miss	skip
tension	gauge
yarn over hook (yoh)	yarn over (yo)

Do you see the difference? The UK doesn't use the term single crochet; single crochet is called a double, and double crochet is called a treble. The treble crochet is called a double treble. Reviewing the pattern key can help you to know whether you're working with a British or American pattern, but it's an easy adjustment, especially as you get used to working the pattern.

Chart reading

Here, you'll see an example of a crochet chart. This chart creates a square like the one you might use to make an afghan. The numbers noted on the chart are row numbers, not stitch numbers; however, not all charts will include those.

Crochet charts are used for a variety of different projects and can, with a bit of practice, be more practical and effective than written instructions. Today, more designers are opting for charts or are including both charts and written instructions. For a complex chart, you may want to also use a row counter. A row counter allows you to click or move a bead to track how many rows you've completed. While this isn't typically necessary for a small chart like this one, it can be very helpful for larger charts.

You only need two things to crochet: a ball of yarn or thread and a hook. All stitches are created by wrapping the thread or yarn around the hook. At first, you may find it a bit confusing or difficult to do. However, as you continue to do it, the entire process will be easier for you.

Most patterns begin with a series of loops, also called chains or a slipstitch. Nevertheless, you can easily learn how to create a foundation without using a standard chain. Projects are typically worked in rows wherein you have to switch back and forth.

You can also stitch in rounds wherein you work around a ring of chains and create a geometric figure, such as a circle, hexagon, or square. You can also use a motif or a geometric piece to stitch together and form your crochet project.

Below is an elaborate list of common crochet symbols that are commonly used.

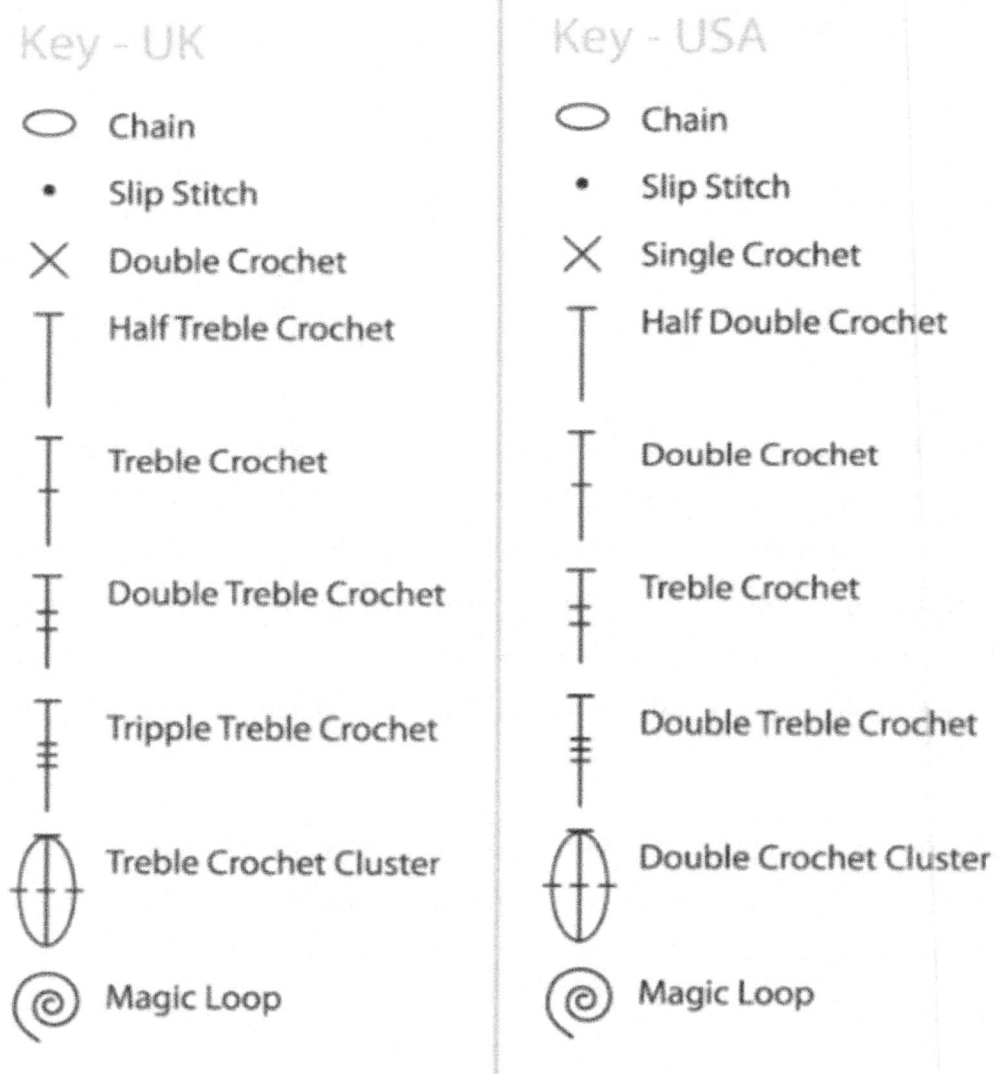

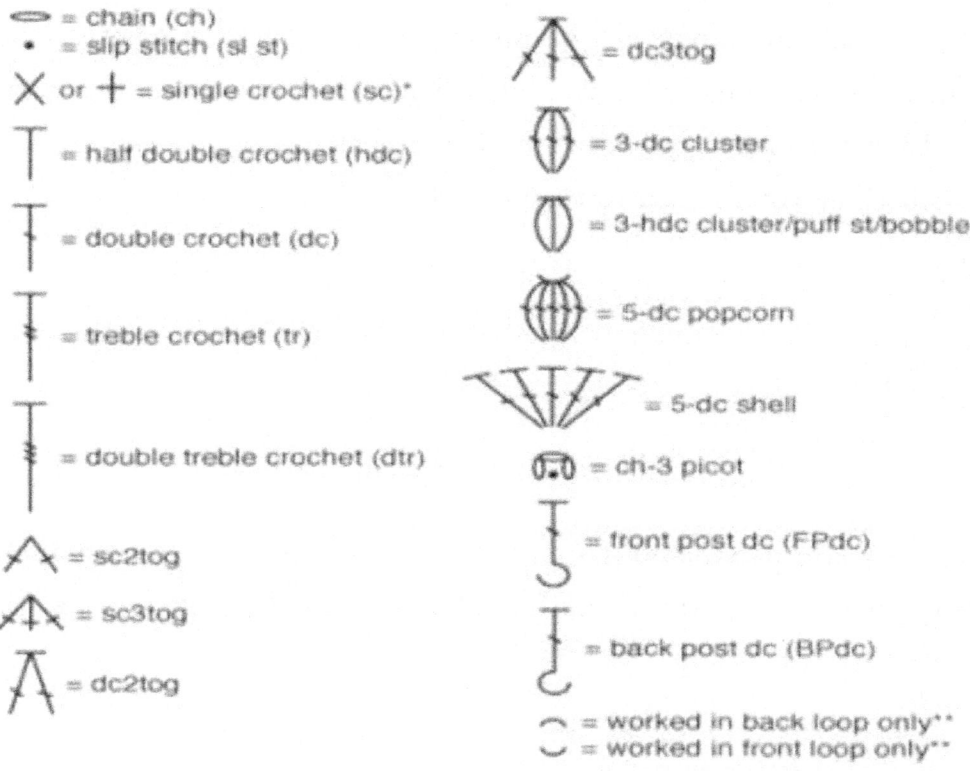

* Both symbols are commonly used for single crochet
** Symbol appears at base of stitch being worked

The keys above illustrates crochet chart symbols. The symbols themselves are universal but do notice that the language refers to American crochet notation and work the stitches accordingly.

Pattern reading

You'll find stitch patterns written in two different ways. The first is the most typical and will be found in vintage patterns, as well as many modern American and British patterns. This is a fully written out stitch pattern, using typical and traditional stitch notation.

Some modern designers in the west, as well as Japanese crochet patterns, do not rely upon written out notation, but on a graphic representation of crochet stitches. These look nothing at all like craft charts you might have used, like those for cross-stitching or knitting. They are, in fact, rather pictorial, with picture symbols written out for each round or row. Once you're used to reading crochet charts, you'll find you can do so with relative ease.

-Charts are much more commonly used for doilies or shawls, rather than simple projects, like a hat or afghan.

-Charts are rarely used for repeated stitch patterns but can be.

Written crochet patterns are still the most common in America and Britain. They are relatively easy to use, and pattern notation is largely standardized.

You may notice something about this chart right away. It creates a visual very similar to the finished work, making it easy to realize what your project should look like, even if you don't have a picture of the finished work.

-Round 1: Ch 16, join with a sl st.

-Round 2: Ch 3, work one dc in the first chain of the last round. *work one dc in thenstitch, 2 dc in thenaround* join with a sl st. (24)

-Round 3: Ch 3, sk 1 dc, sc in next, *ch 3, sk 1 dc, SC in next* join with a sl st.

-Round 4: Ch 3, *1 dc in first sc, sk 1 ch, *10 dc in 2nd ch stitch, sk 1 ch, 1 SC in sc* to last ch 3 loops. 9 dc in 2nd ch st, sl st to join to 3rd ch in initial ch 3.

-Round 5: Sc in 6th dc of last dc cluster, ch 5, dc in sc of prev round, ch5, *sc in 6th dc of the cluster, ch10, dc in sc of prev round, ch 5, dc in sc of prev round, ch5* join with sl st

-Round 6: Working backward to reverse direction, slip stitch in the first 5 ch stitches to the left of your hook. This returns you to the corner of your work. Ch 8, sc in the third ch of ch 5 of the last round. *Ch 5 sc in the third ch of ch 5 of the last round. Ch5, dc 3 in 6th ch of ch 10 of prev round, ch 3, dc3 in the same space*. On the last repeat, dc 2, using the first 3 chains of initial chain 8 to make the third dc. Join with sl st at the third chain.

-Round 7: Working backward again, sl st in first 5 stitches to reach the corner of your work. Ch 8, sc in the third ch of ch 5 of the last round. *Ch 5 sc in the third ch of ch 5 of the last round. Ch5, sc in the third ch of ch 5 of prev round, dc 3 in 6th ch of ch 10 of prev round, ch 3, dc3 in same space*. On the last repeat, dc 2, using the first 3 chains of initial chain 8 to make the third dc. Join with sl st at the third chain.

-Round 8: Working backward again, sl st in first 5 stitches to reach the corner of your work. Ch 8, sc in the third ch of ch 5 of the last round. *Ch 5 sc in the third ch of ch 5 of the last round. Ch5, sc in the third ch of ch 5 of prev round, Ch5, sc in the third ch of ch 5 of prev round, dc 3 in 6th ch of ch 10 of prev round, ch 3, dc3 in same space*. On the last repeat, dc 2, using the first 3 chains of initial chain 8 to make the third dc. Join with sl st at a third chain.

(Note: Rounds 6, 7 and 8 are nearly identical, with the addition of one more ch5 loop per side in each round)

As you can see, that's a very cumbersome pattern written out. It's much easier to follow and understand working from a pictorial chart. This is the benefit of charts for complex and lacy work. If you'd like, you can even make your charts, either by hand or using online charting software.

Chapter 2   Tools and Materials

Take note that if your stitches are too tight or too loose, then your finished project might be slightly different from that of the pattern. If you have tight stitches, you can choose a bigger hook size, and smaller hook size if you have loose stitches – for now. Try to produce even stitches that are not too tight or too loose. Practice makes perfect, and you will surely enjoy every minute of it.

Here are those materials and tools that you need.

Your Yarn or Thread

Crochet yarns come in different categories and thickness, and you need to use the correct hook size according to the thickness of your thread or yarn.

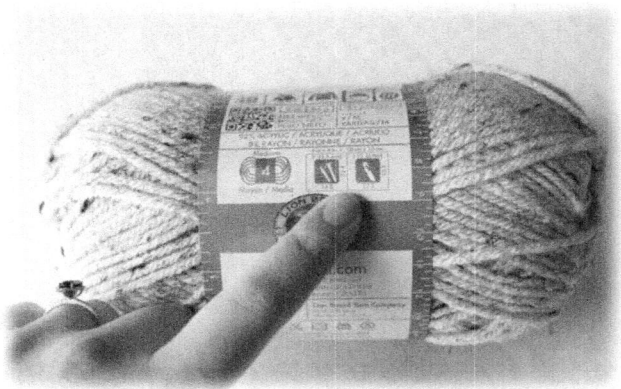

Each ball of yarn comes with a crochet gauge that indicates the number of stitches that you need to make in a number of inches (usually four). In the given chart below, the one used is two instead of four. Assuming that you followed the right hook size to use and the given number was far off the number of stitches on the crochet gauge, it only means that you have a problem with the tension of your stitches.

If you have more stitches than the number of stitches indicated on the crochet gauge, then your stitches are too tight. To create balance, you can use a bigger hook size than the one suggested.

If you have fewer stitches than the number of stitches on the crochet gauge, then your stitches are too loose. You need to use a smaller hook.

Usually, the crochet gauge and the hook size are printed on the yarn label. It is recommended that you choose a cheaper yarn as your practice yarn. It is prudent to choose cheaper yarn since you are still on the learning stage. It is equally wise to choose light colored yarns; you will clearly see your error (just in case) and make necessary adjustments.

The chart in the next page can help you understand and give you an idea about the different crochet yarns and hook size to use.

Crochet Hook and Yarn Weight Chart

Yarn Weight Symbol and Category Name	0 LACE	1 SUPER FINE	2 FINE	3 LIGHT	4 MEDIUM	5 BULKY	6 SUPER BULKY	7 JUMBO
Other Names for Yarn in Category	Fingering, 10 Count, Crochet Thread	Sock, Fingering	Sport, Baby	DK, Light Worsted	Worsted, Afghan, Aran	Chunky, Craft, Rug	Bulky Roving	Jumbo Roving
Recommended Hook Size (US)	Steel[3] 6, 7, 8 Regular B-1	B-1 to E-4	E-4 to 7	7 to I-9	I-9 to K-10.5	K-10.5 to M-13	M-13 to Q	Q And larger
Recommended Hook Size (Metric)	Steel[3] 1.6-1.4 mm Regular 2.25 mm	2.25-3.25 mm	3.5-4.5 mm	4.5-5.5 mm	5.5-6.5 mm	6.5-9 mm	9-15 mm	15 mm and larger
Yards per 50 Gram Roll	275 yds	185-230 yds	145-180 yds	120-142 yds	100-120 yds	85-100 yds	70-85 yds	60 or less yds
Yards per 100 Gram Roll	545 yds	370-460 yds	290-360 yds	240-284 yds	200-240 yds	170-200 yds	140-170 yds	120 or less yds
Number of Single Crochets in 4 Inches[1]	32-42 double crochets[2]	21-32 sts	16-20 sts	12-17 sts	11-14 sts	8-11 sts	7-9 sts	6 sts and fewer

1 These are Guidelines only. They reflect the most commonly used hook sizes for crochet projects based on yarn category.
2 Lace yarn is usually crocheted on larger hooks to create open lacy patterns. Always follow the gauge stated in your pattern.
3 Steel crochet hooks are sized differently from regular hooks. The higher the number the smaller the hook, reversed from regular hook sizing.

Crochet Hook Size Chart

Here is a chart that can give you an idea of the kind of hook that you can use for each type of yarn. Just focus on the size of the hook (some shafts presented in the chart are longer or shorter than the actual); the shafts of the different hook sizes have the same lengths, depending on the manufacturer.

Crochet Hook Conversion Chart		
Metric	USA	UK
2.00 mm	-	14
2.25 mm	1 / B	13
2.50 mm	-	12
2.75 mm	C	11
3.00 mm	-	11
3.25 mm	D	10
3.50 mm	4 / E	9
3.75 mm	F	-
4.00 mm	6	8
4.25 mm	G	-
4.50 mm	7	7
5.00 mm	8 / H	6
5.50 mm	9 / I	5
6.00 mm	10 / J	4
6.50 mm	10 1/2 / K	3
7.00 mm	-	2
8.00 mm	-	0
9.00 mm	15 / N	00
10.00 mm	P	000
15.75 mm or 16mm	Q	-

Steel Hook Chart (thread hooks)		
Metric	USA	UK
.6 mm	14	6
.75 mm	13	-
.70 mm	12	5
.8 mm	11	-
1 mm	10	4
1.15 mm	9	-
1.25 mm	8	3
1.50 mm	7	2.5
1.6 mm	6	-
1.7 mm	5	-
1.75 mm	4	2
1.85 mm	3	-
1.95 mm	2	-
2 mm	1	1
2.25 mm	0	00
3 mm	00	-

Steel and aluminum are the usual materials for the hook. There are some crochet hooks that come in bamboo, plastic, and combinations of the different materials. You can choose any hook material, but just make sure that you choose the hook with a nice hold.

There are cheap crochet hooks and there are expensive crochet hooks with fancy designs, but it is best to start with a cheap hook.

Choosing your Crochet Hook

As mentioned before, a novice should choose the F, G, H, or I U.S. hook size, and fine to medium thread. Look at the crochet hook size chart to see the different hook sizes and their material. First, take a detour in learning the proper way to hold your hook and the different grips.

Types of Crochet Hooks

So, you've seen the chart, and the grips. But what really are these hooks about, and what else should you know about them? Read on and find out!

1. ***Aluminum***. Aluminum Hooks are quite flexible. They are available in a vast amount of sizes, and make crocheting quickly, and smooth!

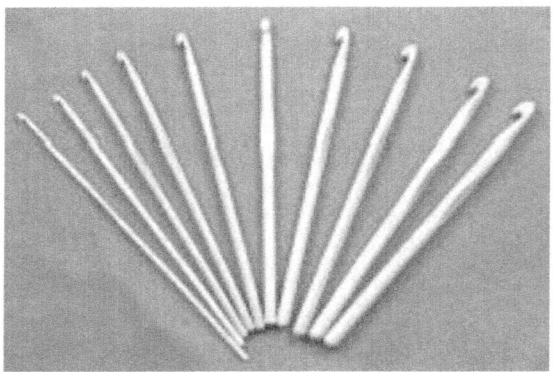

2. ***Steel***. Steel Hooks are known to be best used for small objects, and are often partnered with fine thread. Steel hooks are also known as thread hooks. Examples of crafts you could make with them include doilies, and handkerchiefs.

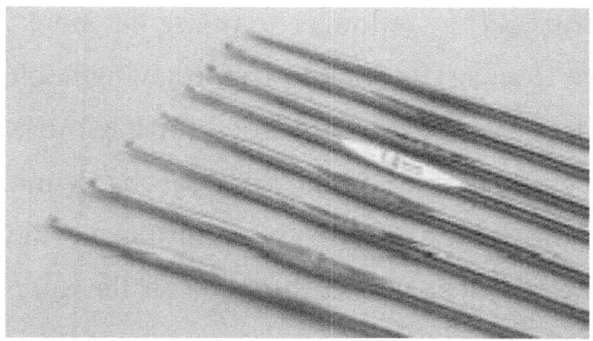

3. **Bamboo**. Meanwhile, bamboo hooks are known to be warm and lightweight. They could either be small, or large, never in between.

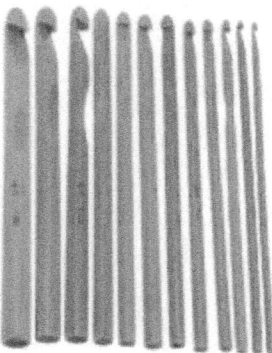

4. **Plastic**. Plastic Hooks could often be common sized or jumbo. They're usually made with plastic that's hollow, and are also lightweight.

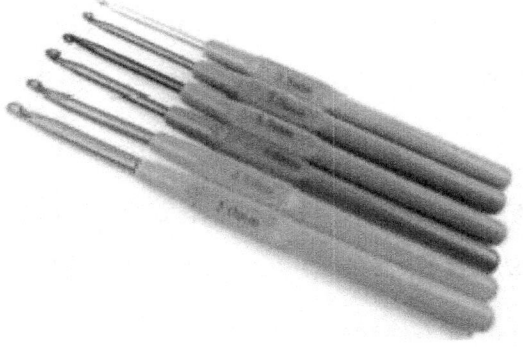

5. ***Tunisian***. Finally, you have Tunisian Hooks. They're longer than regular hooks. Sometimes, Tunisian Hooks are called Cro Hooks. They're known for having hooks on both ends, and that's why they're sometimes not recommended for beginners. Tunisian Hooks are usually used to make crafts that are in the same mechanism as knitted projects. This means that the fabric doesn't look the same as normal crocheted projects do. This is because the stitches stay on the hook while you're making the project, instead of being on the canvas itself.

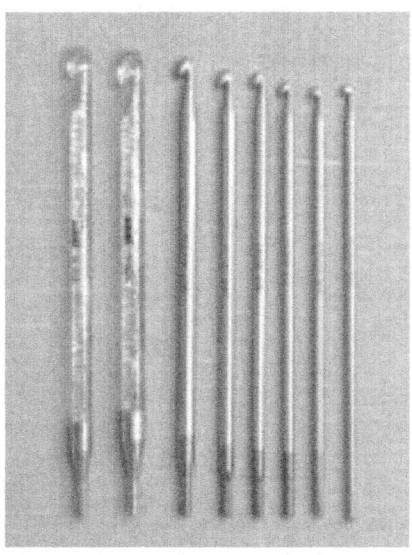

Things to Remember

1. Remember that crochet hook sizes are not universal. This is why you have metric, U.S., and English sizes, and others, too. Remember that size always depends on the country where the hooks were made, the brand, and the material, as well.

2. Size is often determined by the shaft's diameter. The shaft is the point between the needle, and the hook. This will then help you understand how big your stitches shall be.

3. Best thing to keep in mind about size is that hooks made in the United States are represented by letters in their sizes. The farther the letter in the alphabet, the larger the hooks get.

4. Remember that steel hooks best work with lace thread. Take note that as the number gets smaller, the hooks get larger.

Tapestry Needle

There are projects that require you to sew your work, and you will need a tapestry needle for that. You can also use the tapestry needle to sew a crocheted appliqué to your project if it can make the project more appealing. The needle is typically larger than the average needle for sewing and has a rounded (blunt) tip. It has a threading eye to accommodate any yarn, although it may not work for bulky threads.

While often used for cross-stitching, tapestry needles prove to be useful for crocheted materials, too, especially if you need to put on more detail on your project.

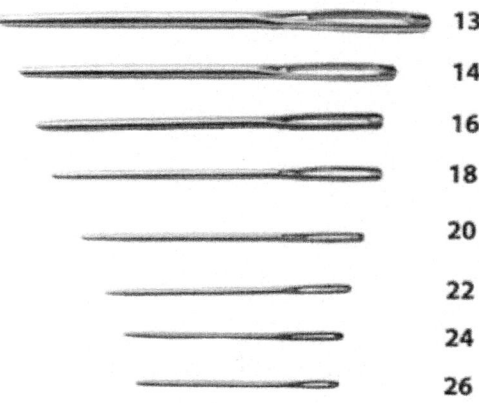

As you may have noticed, the larger the needle, the smaller the number gets—so don't get confused into buying a largely numbered needle thinking it would be a small-sized one.

Choosing Tapestry Needles

Now, you may wonder how exactly you'd choose your tapestry needles. Well, general rule of thumb here is to make sure that you use the kind of needles that will easily accommodate whatever yarn or thread you're currently working with. This means that you'd have to use the smallest needle available, but not necessarily the smallest one out of all sizes, because this would do nothing good for your fabric.

Scissors

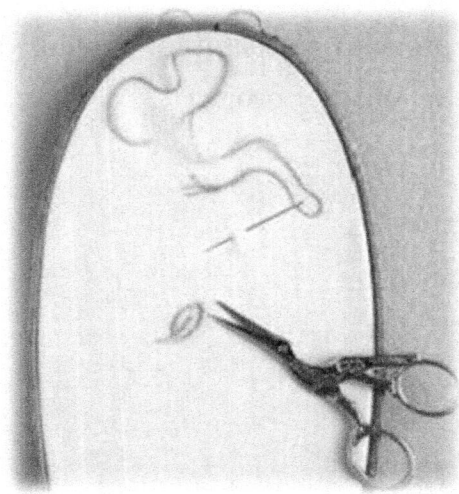

To give your thread a clean cut, you need a pair of scissors. It does not need to be an expensive pair, just the one that is sharp enough to cut your thread without trouble. Make sure to maintain your scissors properly.

As for crochet scissors, one of the most recommended ones are Stork Embroidery Scissors. They're amazing because they do not leave unhinged threads on your project, and would definitely make your crafts neat as could be. Even stitches in front of your fabric will be neatly removed. A sample is shown below.

Stitch Markers

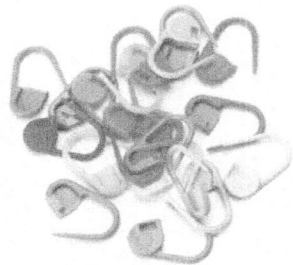

The usual stitch markers look like key holders, paper clips, small plastic hoops, and tiny padlocks. The markers are useful in keeping track of the start or end of a round in the pattern with repetitive instructions. The marker can also serve as reminder of the number of stitches that you made so far. You can also use the markers to keep track of the round that you are currently crocheting.

You can use improvised markers like pieces of thread that you can loosely tie around the post of your stitches on your current round, safety pins, and/or plastic rings. You can use different combinations of materials to mark different rounds

Crochet Hook Case

Your most important tool is your hook. It is best to keep your hook inside a case to avoid possible damage to the tip. There will come a time when simple patterns are not enough to hone your craft. There are projects that only work well with a certain type of yarn and you will need a different hook for that. You might even find yourself owning more than two hooks and you need to store them in a case and keep them organized.

Chapter 3   How to Crochet

Where to put the crochet hook

There are a wide variety of places in a chain where you can place the crochet hook.

Below is a picture of what the top of a chain looks like along with what the top of a single crochet looks like. There are two distinctive loops on each. When crocheting any stitch unless specified by the pattern you will always use both of these loops.

You will insert your hook through both of these loops; this should look similar to the following picture:

Further on into this guide we will cover how to utilize both of those loops in different ways. The only time the placement of your hook can differ is when you start your work off. All projects start with a chain, now as specified above you can indeed go through both loops when working with the chain. However, it may be easier for beginners to just practice by going through one of the loops only. This makes the chain easier to work with, as it can get a little fiddly when you've just started.

How to chain

Chains are the most-common way to start your project. Chains are your first initial building block that you use to guide the rest of your work, and luckily, it is also one of the easiest crochet techniques.

To chain, begin with your knot on the hook holding your yarn gently, slide your hook up and wrap it round the yarn as shown below:

Through the loop, now slide the yarn back down already on the crochet hook and pull. The original knot should come off of your hook and be underneath your first stitch.

To get the required amount of chain stitches, continue to repeat these steps

How to do a single crochet

Single crochet is one of the most-used stitches. It the first basic full stitch you will learn as it is very simple to complete, and many patterns can be made entirely of this one type of crochet stitch.

To make a single crochet, insert your crochet hook in the beginning chain:

Wrap the yarn on the hook, in the same way you would with a chain, pull the yarn back through the stitch but do not go through the loop you already have on the hook, you should now have two loops on hook:

Now wrap the yarn back around the hook without going through a stitch and through the two loops, pull it.

That is a basic single crochet, repeat these steps as required to reach where the row ends.

How to do a turn on your work?

When you reach the end of a row of stitches and need to go the other way, you cannot simply turn it around and keep going. If you were to do this, your work would start to curl in on itself from the tension of not having any slack.

To turn your work, you simply incorporate a single chain where the rows end to do this you chain one simple stitch as shown below once you reach the end of a row.

Once you have this chain, you can turn your work around to face the opposite way and continue your work.

The amount of chains you put where rows stop can vary depending on the type of stitch that you are doing. For example, with single crochet you will usually add one single chain before turning, however with the taller stitches such as double and treble crochet you may add 2-4 chains when you turn.

The amount of chains you need to add when turning is usually written in any good crochet pattern, this can be located at the end of a rows description or if it is the same for every row it may be specified in the pattern description.

How to slip stitch

Slipstitches are an extremely simple form of crochet. This stitch is typically not used to crochet whole projects because it builds up very slowly. It is a very tight stitch that can make your work quite stiff. This type of stitch is frequently found on things like the rim of beanies to make them grip your head better or on projects like pots and bags to add stability and to ensure nothing falls through any gaps.

Slipstitches are also used to get from one side of your project to the other without adding extra rows onto you work. This type of stitch is also commonly used to attach two bits of crochet together as it acts as a type of sewing.

To make a slipstitch, wrapping the yarn round the hook you insert you crochet hook through a stitch and:

Pull it back through your stitch without pulling up a big loop, and then take the yarn through the loop on your crochet hook and repeat as required.

How to do a double crochet

The dc is the hardest stitch that you will learn in this guide, but don't worry with practice it will become easier. The height of a double crochet (dc) is twice that of a single crochet. Fabric made from this stitch is solid and not stiff. This stitch is often used for afghans, sweaters, placemats and shawls. It is also a popular stitch for decorative items for the home.

The dc is essentially the same as a single crochet with an extra few easy steps. The main difference in their appearance is that the dc is considerably taller than a single crochet, which means that this stitch can make your work grow very fast as the stitches you are using are larger.

Another difference in their appearance is how they look altogether, single crochet stitches are very close together which creates a block of fabric which you can barely see through, double crochet, on the other hand, is a lot more open. This means that there will be gaps in your work, because of this; double crochet is a popular choice for granny squares "which intentionally have gaps in them" or lightweight scarves and blankets.

To begin, instead of putting your yarn into a stitch, wrap the yarn across the hook instead. This should leave you with two strands or loops of wool on a hook.

Into the stitch, now insert your hook and pull the yarn through in the same way as you would with a single crochet that should leave you with three twists on a hook.

Now yarn over and through it, pull only 2 of the loops which are on the hook, yarn over once again and pull in the remaining loop.

And there you go! One completed double crochet stitch.

How to make a slipknot

No matter how simple or fancy a crochet project is, everything starts with the slipknot.

- Take the tail end of the yarn and pull out approximately 10-12 inches.

- Make a small loop with the tail end. Fold the working end (end of the yarn connected to the rest of the ball) of the yarn over the tail end (cut end) to form an x. Pinch the bottom of this loop.

- About 2 inches away from the first loop, make another loop (smaller loop). Pinch the bottom, too.

- Insert the 2nd (smaller loop) into the 1st loop.

- Pull the loop tight but leave enough room for the crocheting hook.

- Into the loop, put the hook. Pull the loop until the hook is snug between it.

Chain Stitch (ch)

The chain stitch is one the basic stitches in crochet. this is often used as the starting or foundation chain.

- Hold the crochet hook comfortably with the dominant hand.

- Make a slipknot.

- With the hook on the slipknot, make a yarn over and pull it via the slipknot. This is the 1st chain stitch.

- Repeat the above step until the number of required chain stitches is made.

- Keep the last loop of the chain stitch on the hook before proceeding.

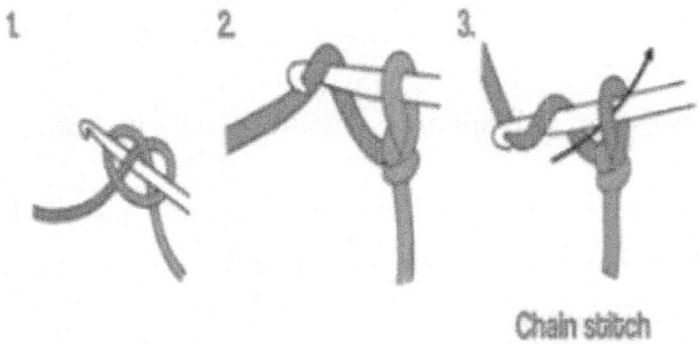

Chain stitch

Half-Double Crochet (hdc)

Half-double crochet provides a good texture to crochet fabric. It also adds appeal to the crochet work. The height is somewhere in between the single crochet and the double crochet. The fabric it produced is fairly tight, like one made with single crochet.

1. Begin with a row of chain stitches. Keep the last loop on the chain.

2. Start a half double crochet on the 3rd chain from the hook. The 1st 2 chains will count as the 1st hdc.

3. Over the hook, wrap the yarn.

4. Skip the 1st 2 chain stitches and put the hook into the 3rd one.

5. Once inserted, use the hook to grab the yarn and make a yarn over.

6. through the loop, pull the yarn of the chain stitch. There should be 3 loops resting on the crochet hook.

7. Make another yarn over by wrapping the yarn over the hook. Pull the yarn through all of the 3 loops onto the crochet hook. One hdc has just been made.

8. Repeat the steps until all the chain stitches have been used.

9. When reaching the row's end, make 1 last hdc then 2 chain stitches. The chain stitches will be the turning chain.

Double Triple Crochet (dtr)

This stitch creates a loose fabric full of large holes. This is more often used when creating lace designs such as doilies. Other crochet patterns using fine cotton are ideal for this type of crochet stitch.

1. Create a foundation chain of 15 ch.

2. Add 5 ch more for the turning chain.

3. Perform 3 yarn overs and put the hook into the center of the 6th chain after the hook.

4. Perform 1 yo and pull it through the chain stitch's center.

5. Make 1 yo and on the crochet hook, pull it through the 1st 2 loops.

6. Continue making 1 yarn over and pulling it through the 2 loops until only 1 loop is left on the hook. One dtr has just been made.

7. Make another 3 yo to begin another dtr. Continue until all ch in the foundation have been stitched.

8. When all ch is done, make 5 ch for the turning chain. Make 3 yo and insert into the 2nd dtr of the 1st row.

9. Continue along each dtr of the 1st row.

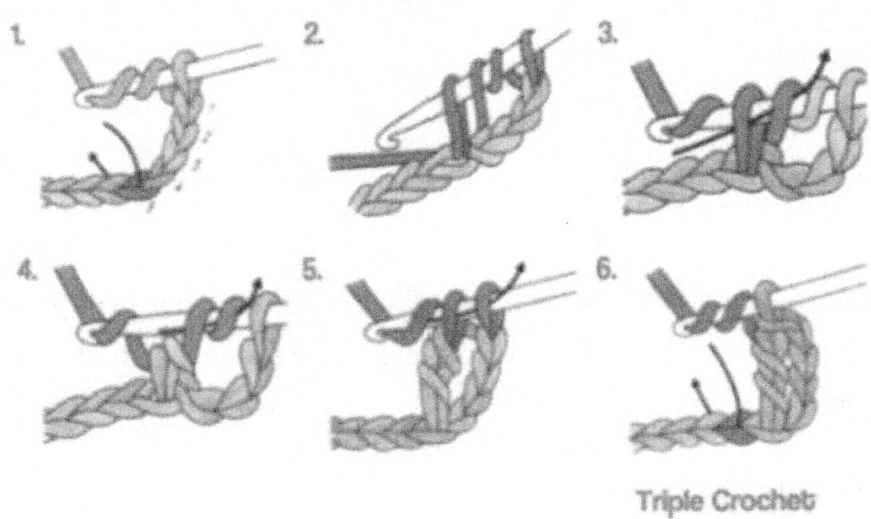

Triple Crochet

Chapter 4   Patterns

Granny Square

<u>Skill Level</u>: *Beginner*

This is a prevalent crochet pattern, and you will find great value in knowing how to go through it.

You will begin by creating the slipknot and then creating three chains. Then you start using the double crochet so that you end up with double stitches. Then once you do this, loop the two double stitches through the third chain.

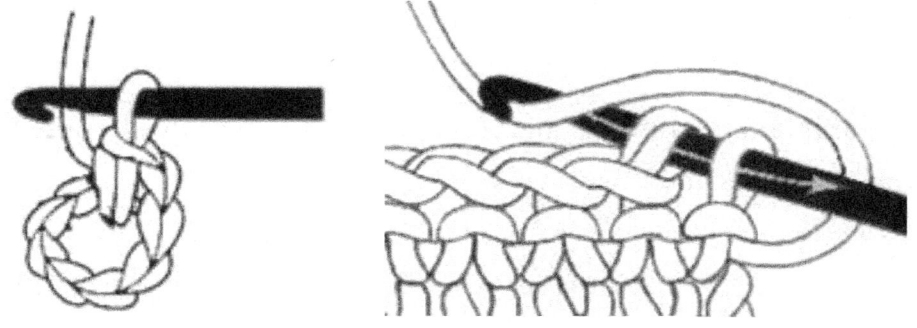

Then after this, create another three of such dc clusters so that, but now you will move the dc into the foundation of the first round.

Then, repeat the first two steps. Then, repeat this process, beginning with a new foundation chain from the end of one dc stitch as you create the stitching until you get to the size of the granny square that you want.

You will then use the granny square on whatever you may want, from small tablemats to covers for items in the house such as sound systems and TV sets. Depending on how you have woven it, you can also use it as a cover for pillows or small furniture like stools.

This is an example of a granny square. As we see, it alternates between sc and dc, as well as loops on chains and rows.

Shell or Fan Pattern Stitches

<u>Skill Level</u>: *Beginner*

The shell or fan line is one of the most prominent structures for child covers, tosses, and afghans. A shell is a gathering of three to five lines worked into a solitary fastens or chain space. The gathering will be nearer together at the base and spread out at the top, so each gathering resembles a fan or seashell.

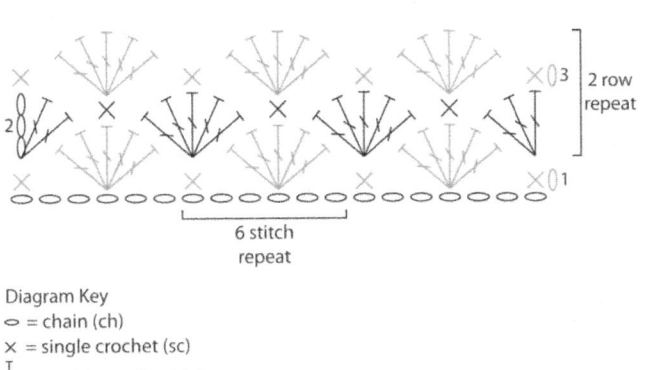

To create the shell stitch, you will make multiple chains of six stitches or if you want to use the stitch as an edging, you will count in sixes for the number of shells you will make and you will add one more chain. The first two chains from the hook will count as one double crochet (dc). Then, you will work five dc into the third chain.

The set of five dc actually creates the shell effect. To secure the first shell, you will skip two chain stitches and work a single crochet (sc) into the chain stitch after. So, to complete the row, you will repeat the following: skip two stitches, work five dc into the third stitch, skip two stitches, and work a sc into the sixth stitch.

You will repeat this until the end of the row, ending with a sc. If you work only one row of sc, it would make a wonderful edging, but you can also work in multiple rows and create something bigger, like a blanket or a pillowcase.

Crochet with Plastic Rings

Skill Level: *Beginner*

Pure fun brings crocheting with plastic rings. A brisk job that brings results quickly. However, you should not crochet the rings individually but create coherent chains.

To start, put the normal crochet start loop on the plastic ring. The loop for the first solid ash and all subsequent hands is always pulled through the ring. Then, as usual, the two loops that are on the needle are embraced with an envelope.

Repeat this until the ring is completely crocheted. Before you start work, crochet a ring completely to the sample to know how many units are needed overall. This is also dependent on wool strength.

Connect Rings Together

The connection between two rings takes place when the first plastic ring is crocheted in half with solid hands. Now, crochet an air mesh and then the first solid mesh around the next ring.

The last ring of a row is always completely crocheted. All other half-finished crocheted rings will be completed in the second round with solid hands. In doing so, always crochet a solid piece of ash around the connecting air mesh. In the end, pull the thread through the last stitch and sew it.

The second row of rings can now also be half crocheted and connected to the rings of the first row. When crocheting the first half of the second row of rings, add the already finished first row of rings. To do this, crochet a slit stitch into the middle stitch of the already finished ring row.

The crochet with plastic rings is particularly suitable for original placemats, small coasters, and the design of fabric bags, which receive such a special design. Of course, all these suggestions are also suitable for individual gifts.

Group Crochet Stitch Patterns

Skill Level: *Beginner*

The best-realized group join is presumably the bobble line. The bobble is more often than not between a couple of single knit lines and is made by doing a yarn over, embedding the sew guide into the bobble's base fasten, and hauling a circle out.

This is rehashed multiple times in the base fasten, bringing about six circles staying on the snare. The yarn is dismantled through each of the six circles to make the bobble, at that point verified by making a solitary knit in the fasten that tails it.

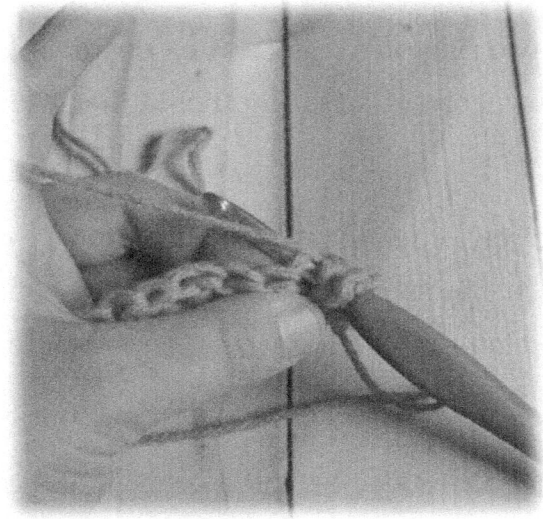

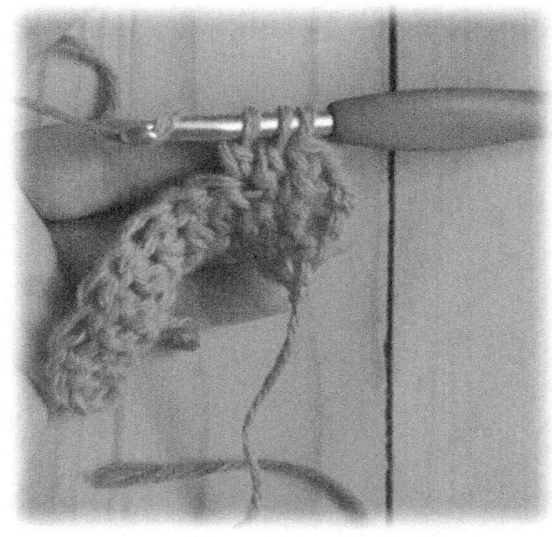

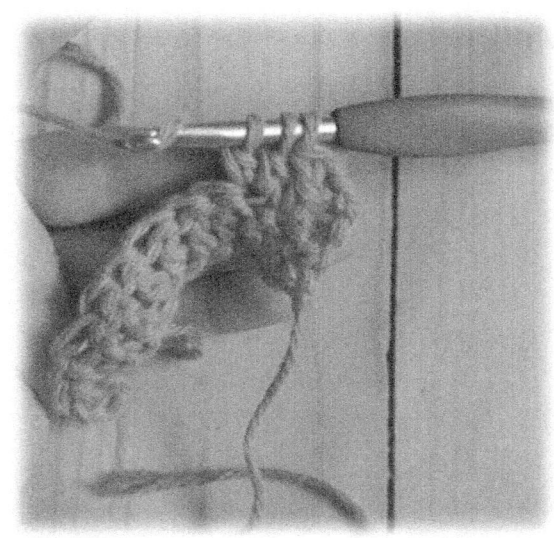

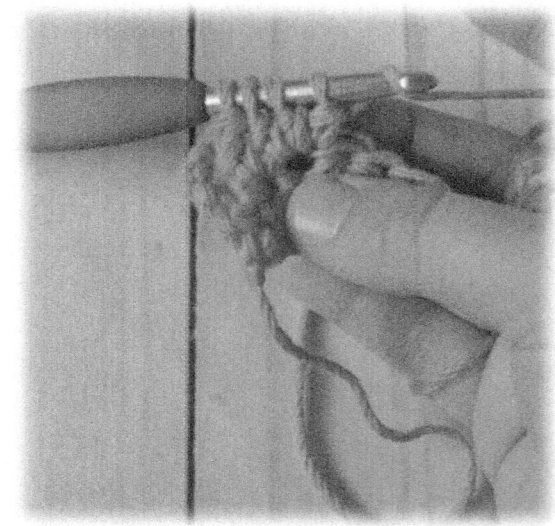

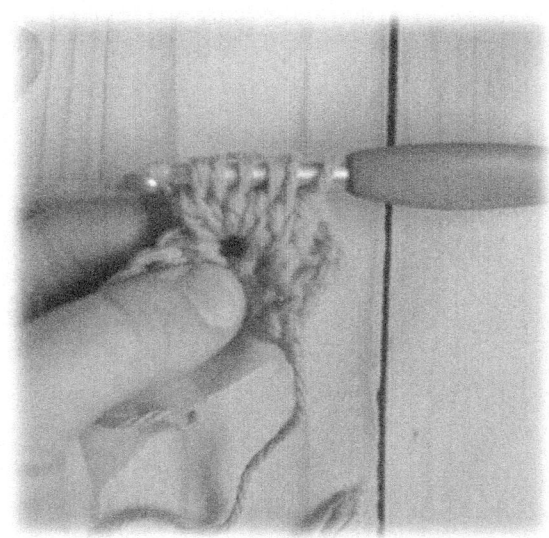

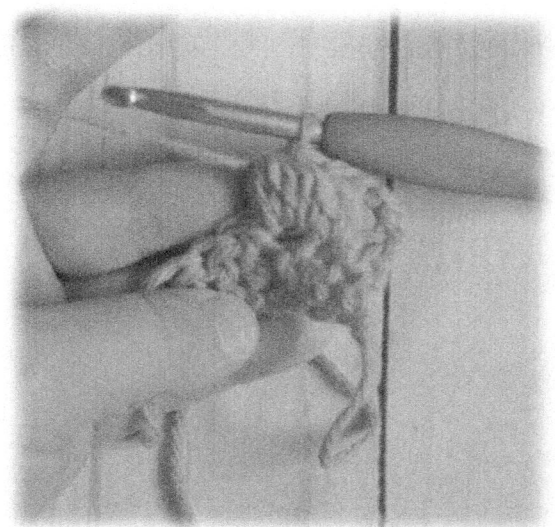

Another prevalent group example is the pineapple line.

Chipped away at a different of two in addition to four, the pineapple is made by doing a yarn over, embedding the sew snare in a solitary line, and pulling up a circle multiple times, making a yarn over. Draw the sew yarn through eight circles at that point make another yarn over and pull the yarn through the last two circles. In contrast to bobbles, pineapples are not normally moored with single-knit lines.

Rather, a join is skipped between every pineapple, and a chain is made over the skipped fasten. In the following line, the pineapples are made in the chain space between the pineapples on the last column. The highest point of the pineapple is skipped, and a chain is made above it.

Valentine's Heart

Skill Level: *Beginner*

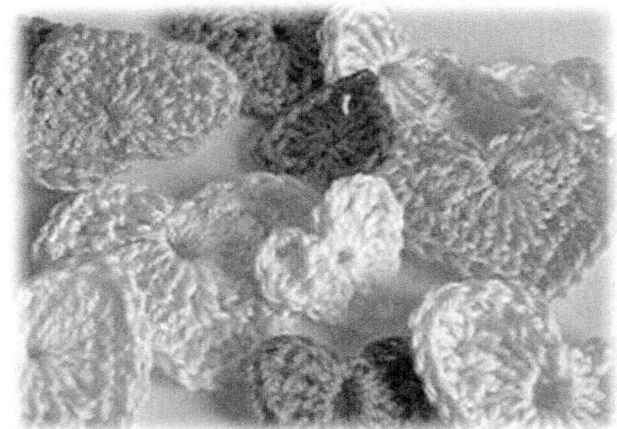

Yarn: Lightweight yarn.

Needle: D.

Tools: Crochet hook, tapestry needle.

Pattern Instructions:

Row 1: Ch 2, 15 dc into ring, sl st into top of first dc.

Row 2: Ch 2, 1 dc into same st, 4 trc into next stitch, 2 dc into next st, 1 hdc into each of next 4 sts.

Row 3: 1 dc, 1 trc, 1 dc into next st.

Row 4: 1 hdc into each of next 4 sts, 2 dc into next st, 4 trc into next st, 1 dc into next st, ch 2, sl st into same st.

Fasten off and weave in ends.

Spiral Flowers

Skill Level: Advanced

Yarn: Light weight yarn.

Needle: B.

Tools: Crochet hook.

Pattern Instructions:

Row 1: Ch 4. Join with slst to first chain to form a ring.

Row 2: Ch 7. Slst in 2nd chain from hook and in each of the remaining 5 chains. Slst into center of ring. Turn your work 180 degrees clockwise. Do not flip. Slst into center of ring.

Working in the back loops only: Sc into first stitch. Hdc 2 into the second stitch. Hdc into third stitch. Dc 2 into fourth stitch. Dc into fifth stitch. Dc into sixth stitch.

Ch 2 and turn your work.

Working in the back loops only: Slst into each of the next 8 stitches. Slst into center of ring.

Petal Instructions:

Row 1: Ch 1 and turn your work.

Working into the front loops from the previous petal:

Sc into first stitch. Hdc 2 into the second stitch. Hdc into third stitch. Dc 2 into fourth stitch. Dc into fifth stitch. Dc into sixth stitch. You will have two stitches remaining, do not work into these stitches.

Row 2: Ch 2 and turn your work.

Working in the back loops only: Slst into each of the next 8 stitches. Slst into center of ring.

Repeat the Petal Instructions 9 times to give you 11 petals.

Finish off and weave in your ends.

Rainbow Fold-Over Coin Purse

Easy, simple, and eye catching—talk about aesthetical and functional. Have fun making this in rainbow shades, gradient shades, or alternate between your favorite colors.

Note: This works well with any kind of yarn, just make sure you use the appropriate hook according to the yarn's thickness.

1st Round

1. Make a Magic Ring.
2. Make 3 Chains and 12 DCs into the Magic Ring.
3. Slip stitch into the 1st stitch you made and fasten off. You should have 13 stitches in total.

2nd Round

Change yarn color.

1. Make a DC into one of the stitches from the previous row. Pass in a 2nd DC into the same stitch.

2. Finish this round by making 2 DCs in each stitch from the previous round.

3. Slip stitch into the 1st stitch you made and fasten off. You should have 26 DCs in total.

3rd Round

Change yarn color.

1. Start with 1 DC into any stitch from the previous round.

2. In the next stitch, make 2 DCs into the same stitch, and make 1 DC in the next stitch.

3. Repeat step 2 until you finish this round, alternating between 2 DCs and 1 DC.

4. Slip stitch into your 1st stitch and fasten off. You should have 39 DCs.

4th Round

Change yarn color.

1. Make two DCs in two separate stitches.

2. Make 2 DCs into one stitch.

3. Repeat steps 1 and 2 until you finish this round, alternating between 2 DCs in two separate stitches and one 2 DCs in the same stitch.

4. Slip stitch into the 1st stitch you made and fasten off. You should have 52 DCs.

5th Round

Change yarn color.

1. In this round, make 3 DCs in three separate stitches, and stitch in 2 DCs into the 4th stitch.

2. Keep alternating between 3 DCs in three separate stitches, and stitch in 2 DCs into the 4th stitch

3. Slipstitch into the first stitch you made and fasten off. You should have 65 DCs.

6th Round

Change yarn color.

1. In this round, make 4 DCs in three separate stitches, and stitch in 2 DCs into the 5th stitch.

2. Keep alternating between 4 DCs in three separate stitches, and stitch in 2 DCs into the 5th stitch

3. Slipstitch into the first stitch you made and fasten off. You should have 78 DCs.

7th Round

Change yarn color.

1. In this round, make 5 DCs in three separate stitches, and stitch in 2 DCs into the 6th stitch.

2. Keep alternating between 5 DCs in three separate stitches, and stitch in 2 DCs into the 6th stitch

3. Slipstitch into the first stitch you made and fasten off. You should have 91 DCs.

How to Assemble

1. With a needle and thread, sew in a zipper on half of the circle.

2. Fold over, and sew in the other half onto the other side of the zipper.

3. Embellish with beads and sequins or leave as is.

Chapter 5   Types Of Crochet

Afghan Stitch Coaster

It's a small thing but a coaster can go a long way and makes for a fun small project and handmade gift. This pattern also features the long single crochet. To do this insert the hook into the stitch, yarn over, and draw a loop through to have two loops on the hook. Yarn over again, draw through both loops on the hook. These are really just regular single stitches but worked in a row that isn't the regular working row.

You need white and green worsted weight wool and a size G Tunisian crochet hook.

Row 1: Use the white wool to chain 14, draw up a loop in the second chain from the hook. Draw up a loop in each remaining chain. Yarn over and draw through the one loop.

Row 2-12: Draw up a loop in each vertical bar to get 14 loops on your hook. Yarn over, draw through one loop.

Don't fasten off right now.

Now to work the border.

Row 1: Use the soft white to chain 1, sc evenly around the entire coaster base (use the pattern sc, chain 1, sc) in each corner stitch. Now you fasten off.

Row 2: Join the green yarn in any stitch you want. Sc in some of the places you placed the single stitches in row one, working the singles as you go. Sc in each sc, with three sc in each corner.

Fasten off and you're done.

Amigurumi Crochet

This type of crochet is said to have originated from Japan. People would use this type of crochet when making toys that would be stuffed using this crochet. Ami means knitting or yarn that has been crocheted while amigurumi means a doll that has been stuffed.

This type of crochet is therefore used when one is making these stuffed dolls through the use of heavy yarn. One can also make fan items and the large novelty cushions as well as the homewares.

Flower Madala

Crochet Hook: 6.5mm or K/10.5

Weight of Yarn: Bulky Yarn (5) (12 to 15 stitches for four inches)

Round 1: With the first color, chain 2. Work 10 half-double-crochet in 2nd chain from hook. Join. (10 stitches)

Round 2: ch 1. Work 2 single crochet in each st around. Join. (20 stitches)

Round 3: chain 1. *Work 3 double crochet in subsequent st. Skip 1 st*. Replicate (*) around. Join. (30 stitches, or ten "clusters")

Round 4: ch 1. Working between the clusters for this round, *double crochet, three treble crochet, double crochet*. Replicate (*) around. Join. (50 stitches)

Round 5: Slip stitches over to the 2nd treble crochet. Chain 1. Single crochet in top of center treble crochet. Chain 5. *Skip subsequent four stitches. Single crochet in top of subsequent center treble crochet. Ch 5*. Replicate (*) around. Join. (10 stitches + 10 chain 5 spaces)

Round 6: ch 1. *Single crochet in single crochet st. Work {2 double crochet, treble crochet, ch 1. slip stitch in top of treble crochet just worked, treble crochet, two double crochet} in subsequent chain five space*. Replicate (*) around. Join. Tie-up and weave all ends.

Aran Crochet

This is a type of crochet that is normally ribbed and also one that is cabled. It is a traditional type of crochet which is made through interlocking cables. Through this type of crocheting, one can make sweaters and chunky beanies as well as scarves.

This type of crocheting is said to produce very strong items as a result of the interlocking of the cables. This is the reason why people use it to make items that would need to be worn for longer periods of time. They can also be used to make blankets and Afghans as well as jackets and coats and also scarves.

Bavarian Crochet

This is a type of crochet which is said to work just like the granny squares, which were traditionally made. It is used when one wants to make very thick items and also when they want to blend in different colors when making them.

This type of crochet is said to allow people to be able to blend in different colors without experiencing any challenges. They are able to do this by working on each part on its own. This helps them to be able to blend them together, which makes them come up with a very fancy item. The granny squares make it very appealing since one can even use squares of different colors. One can make blankets and shawls through the use of Bavarian crochet.

Bosnian Crochet

Bosnian crochet is used when one wants to make a dense and knit like material through the use of a crochet slip sew up. One has to, however, stitch different parts of a stitch on the current row. One has to ensure that the stitches are different in each row. They are able to achieve this through the use of the Bosnian crochet hooks, which are said to produce very good crochets. One can still work with the normal hooks; even the Bosnian hooks give better crochets than the other hooks.

This type of crochet is not very popular. This is because one would think that it is normal knitting when you look at the crochet. It is easy to work with it since the style used is easy to learn. People use it when one is making the scarves and beanies, as well as when crocheting items that do not require much time to be crocheted.

Bullion Crochet

This is a type of crochet that requires one to use a lot of time when making them. One uses many wraps of the yarn, which have to be put around a hook that is very long. By doing this, one is able to come up with a very unique stitch. This type of crochet is used when one needs to make the motifs and not when making crochets that require one to use the fabrics.

It takes a lot of time to produce the item you are making using this type of crochet since one has to be very keen when coming up with the patterns. The final product is normally very firm and thick, as well as stiff. A crocheter uses a method to make items that are meant to be long-lasting. One can make mats and stiff materials when they use this type of crocheting. This helps them to be able to come up with materials that are very unique and firm, so they can be used for a very long time without them wearing out.

Broomstick Crochet

This type of crochet is also called jiffy lace. It is normally made through the use of traditional crochet hooks. One forms make some stitches all round a very long as well as wide stick that looks like that one of a broomstick.

In this modern age, people are said to use the large crochet hooks as well as the thick dowel when they are making the broomstick lace nowadays. It is a skill that people need to take their time to learn in order for them to come up with a well-made crochet.

It is, however, a type of crochet that is said to produce crochets that are very beautiful and unique. One can make baby shawls using this type of crochet and also throw blankets that are normally used for the purposes of decoration.

Bruges Crochet

This is a type of crochet that is used when one wants to make Bruges laces, as the name suggests. One first creates ribbons meant for the crochet, which are sewed together in order for them to form the desired lace pattern.

They are said to form very beautiful patterns that are also unique. This is because they are neatly sewed together. One can use different colors when making these patterns, which makes them even more beautiful. This type of crochet is used for making table mats and shawls as well as embellishments that are used for clothing.

Clothesline Crochet

This is a type of crochet which is said to utilize the stitches that were used traditionally. One uses a very thick yarn when making items using this type of crochet. They work on a rope that has to be very thick since when making mats, one requires something that will be so strong and which will be easy to style as well as shape.

This type of crocheting is mostly used when one is making mats and baskets or anything that is required to be strong. One needs to have skills on how to make items using this type of crochet since they need to make first make the item they need to make on the ground before they can crochet it. This type of crochet is used in the making of mats and baskets as well as wall hangings.

Clones Lace Crochet

This type of crochet was said to be easy to make in the past and was very popular among people who love crocheting. It resembled the Irish lace, which was made because it was so easy to make. Clones knots are made, which makes as they are normally part of the crocheting process. One needs to learn this skill in order for them to ensure that they know how to make items using it. This type of crochet is used when one is making delicate dresses that require one to be very keen.

Filet Crochet

This crochet is a style that is achieved through the use of chains as well as double crochets. One achieves a crochet that has a pattern that is grid-like, which can be filled or left without filling. The space that is left is used in the creation of desired pictures which have to be included in the design. It creates patterns that are so unique and are neatly embedded within the crochet. This is something that is so unique about this type of crochet. All the squares that are left empty when crocheting may be filled with pictures of one desire. This type of crocheting is used when one is making the baby blankets, handbags, jackets, and kimonos, as well as when they are making cushions.

Finger Crochet

Finger crocheting is practiced when one barely uses the hook when crocheting. It is used when one is making some hand fabrics. During this type of crocheting, one will mostly use their hands to crochet.

The patterns are fixed together to come up with one complete item. When one is making fabrics using this type of crochet, one cannot do it too fast. They will spend a lot of time crocheting, which may make them make very few items for a very long period of time. One can only make some string bags and small scarves which do not require much time when making them.

Hairpin Crochet

This is a type of crochet that is said to work just like the broomstick crochet even though in the past, people used crochet hooks. Pieces being crocheted were held together through the use of metals that were then. One is able to get very beautiful and unique crochets that are well finished. They are used when one is making shawls and wraps as well as scarves.

Chapter 6   Types Of Projects

Friendship Bracelet

Crochet friendship bands are a simple group gift that works up really quickly and easily. And, the best part, it fits every age. If someone doesn't like to wear a friendship bracelet, it can be used as a bookmark or keychain instead. Make the following pattern of friendship band and then tweak it as you like.

Finish size: adult size bracelet

Materials you will need:

1 ball of crochet thread of size 10, 9mm thread

Crochet hook

Scissor

How to do:

Step 1: Take two strands of thread, hold them together, and chain 52 stitches in the size that you want.

Make a two-toned effect and for this, turn the chain and then work in half double crochet (hdc) across the row in each chain.

Step 2: Work on the last row of crochet, and for this, turn the bracelet and slip stitch (sl st) in back loop only (BLO) of each half double crochet (hdc) in step 1.

Cut off the thread by using a scissor, leave 3 inches of thread at the end and then tie off the thread, don't weave in ends.

Hand Towels

Crochet towels are handy in the kitchen, and they can be used for a variety of purposes, like keeping them near the washing sink. Moreover, hand towels make a great gift with a wooden scrub brush or fun dish soup. So let's get started with the easy crochet instructions to make your own kitchen hand towel.

Finish size: 10.5-by-18 inches (26.5-by-46 centimeters.

Materials you will need:

Ball(s) of knit pick cotlin yarn, depending on the colors you want to prefer. Use more colors to make a striped hand towel.

H crochet hook of 5.5 mm size

Tapestry needle

Scissor

Sewing needle and thread (optional)

Button (optional)

Yarn needle

Gauge: 14 rows and 12 stitches as 4 inches (10 centimeters) in the pattern.

How to do:

To make this crochet hand towel, you should know how to do pique stitch. It is quite simple to work with – just yarn over (yo) and then insert hook into the third chain (ch-3) from the hook; you can also do this from the first stitch (st) of the row.

Yarn over (yo) and then draw a loop. Make three loops on the hook, and your stitch will look like a double crochet stitch (dc). Then yarn over (yo) and draw it through the three loops; in this way, you will have two loops on the hook.

Yarn over (yo) to insert the hook into the same chain, like in the previous step, and draw up a loop; in this way, you will have four loops. It will your first complete pique stitch.

Now, you these instructions for pique stitch to crochet a hand towel.

If you are thinking of making a striped hand towel, here's how you can lose a chain for a starting chain.

Row 1: Starting from the third chain (ch-3), work a pique stitch in every thirty stitches (sts).

Row 2: Single crochet stitch (sc) in every stitch (st). Then work in chain 2 (ch-2) for a turning chain and turn.

Row 3: Now pique stitch in every stitch and then work chain 1 (ch-1) for a turning chain and turn.

1. Repeat row 2, row 3, and row 4 and then change to the new yarn, e.g., color 1.

2. Then repeat row 3 and row 2 two times and change to another color yarn, e.g., color 2.

3. Now, repeat row 3 and row 2 one time and then change to a different color yarn, e.g., color 3.

4. Repeat row 3 and row 2 two times, change to the color 2 yarn, and then repeat row 3 and row 2 one time.

5. Change to a different color yarn, e.g., color 4 and repeat row 3 and row 2 two times.

6. Change to the color 2 yarn and then repeat row 3 and row 2 seven times.

7. Change to the floor 4 yarn and then and then repeat row 3 and row 2 two times.

8. Change to the color 2 yarn and then repeat row 3 and row 2 one time.

9. Change to the color 3 yarn and then repeat row 3 and row 2 two times.

10. Change to the color 2 yarn and then repeat row 3 and row 2 one time.

11. Change to the color 1 yarn and then repeat row 3 and row 2 two times.

12. Change to the color 2 yarn and then repeat row 3 and row 2 three times.

13. Now, you are done; secure the last stitch, trim the yarn and weave in all the ends.

You can also crochet a hanging loop to attach it around the kitchen like on a cabinet handle or hook. For this, make a tail and to make it, when you reach the upper left corner of the towel, slip stitch (sl st) in the 5 chain (ch-5) from the hook to make a button loop.

Then slip stitch (sl st) in the remaining chains and work back towards the kitchen towel. When done, slip stitch (sl st) in the single crochet stitch (sc) at the corner and secure the last stitch and trim it. Now, weave this tail through the two rows of the hand towel and then sew the button. Secure the yarn and weave in loose ends by using a yarn needle.

Phone and Tablet Cover

Do you hate plastic cases for your cell phone or tablet? It's time to give a makeover to your phone cases and giving it better protection. Crocheting patterns for a tablet or cell phone is a great project if you have leftover yarn. It is also quick and adaptable for all of its kinds. You can customize the pattern by measuring according to the phone.

Finish size: the size of the cell phone or tablet

Materials you will need:

250 gram balls of worsted weight yarn (one or two colors)

F crochet hook of 3.75 mm size

Wooden button (about 1 ¾-inch)

Scissor

Yarn needle

Sewing needle and thread (optional)

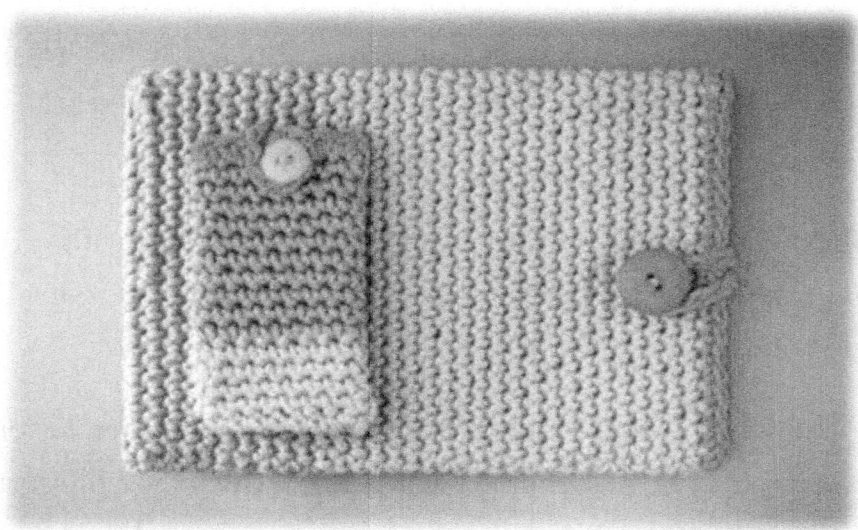

How to do:

This pattern will need front post half-double crochet stitch (phdc). For this, take the hook, wrap yarn around it, and then from the front of the next stitch, insert the hook around the post and then work in half double crochet stitch (hdc).

Round 1: Yarn over (yo), then draw a loop and work in chain 30 (ch-30) to leave a long tail for sewing. If you are using two colors, then crochet the bottom part of the case with one color by first wrapping it around the cell phone or tablet and begin with chain 30 (ch-30). Add 4 more chains to make slipping in and out easy for the cell phone or tablet from the case. For more adjustment, increase or decrease the chains. You can also slip stitch (sl st) the chain 1 (ch-1) to form a ring, don't twist, and then work the rest of the rounds without slip stitching (sl st) or turning at the end of the round.

Round 2: Work in chain 1 (ch-1), then 1 single crochet stitch (sc) in the next chain, and work in each chain till it reaches at the beginning chain 1 (ch-1) in the same chain, don't slip stitch (sl st) or turn.

Round 3: *Work in single crochet stitch (sc) in the next single crochet stitch (sc) and each single crochet stitch (sc) of the round*. Repeat from * to * till the case reaches of the two-third height of the cell phone or tablet. Then even out the edge by slip stitch (sl st) to the next stitch and fasten off.

Turn the crochet case inside out and then shut the bottom seam by sewing it with yarn tail that was made in round 1. When the tail has weaved in, bring the right side outside and then turn the case inside out.

Round 4: Use a new color and join it with a couple of slip stitch (sl st) and then fasten off the point. Work in chain 2 (ch-2) by half double crochet stitch (hdc) over the yarn tail, work in half double crochet stitch (hdc) in the next stitch and each stitch and then slip stitch (sl st) to top of the beginning of chain 2 (ch-2).

Round 5: Work in chain 2 (ch-2) by half double crochet stitch (hdc), and then work the front post half double crochet stitch (fphdc) around the next half double crochet stitch (hdc). *Work in 1 half double crochet stitch (hdc), 1 front post half double crochet stitch (fphdc) around the next half double crochet stitch (hdc)* and then repeat from * to * till the end of the round. When done, slip stitch (sl st) to top of the beginning of chain 2 (ch-2).

Round 6: Work in chain 2 (ch-2) by half double crochet stitch (hdc), and work in front post half double crochet stitch (fphdc) around the next front post half double crochet stitch (fphdc). * Work in 1 half double crochet stitch (hdc) in the next half double crochet stitch (hdc), and front post half double crochet stitch (fphdc) around next front post half double crochet stitch (fphdc)*. Repeat from * to * till the end of the round and then slip stitch (sl st) to top of the beginning of chain 2 (ch-2).

Repeat round 5 until the case is half-inch less than the height of the cell phone or tablet and then insert it in the case to check the measurement.

Round 7: Work in chain 1 (ch-1), then single crochet in next stitch and each stitch around. Work in 1 single crochet stitch (sc) in the same stitch as the beginning of chain 1 (ch-1) and then slip stitch (sl st) to the first single crochet stitch (sc).

Repeat round 6 one more time and, when done, fasten off and insert the cell phone or tablet into the case; it should go fully in.

Round 8: Attach the button and for this, slip stitch (sl st) the button at the top middle of the case, then work in chain 17 (ch-17) and slip stitch (sl st) into the same stitch. Fasten off, knot the ends a couple of times and weave them in by using a needle through the inner layer so that tail doesn't show outside. When done, secure the last stitch, trim it, then secure the yarn and weave in loose ends by using a yarn needle.

That's it! With just seven steps, you can create your own cozy for cell phones or tablets. If you have some yarn left in a different color, try using it in the pattern, crocheting a flower, or personalizing the case even more.

Chapter 7   Mistakes and Solutions

Regardless of whether you are simply learning to crochet or have long periods of experience, we are for the most part liable for committing similar errors. There is no disgrace in succumbing to these regular crochet bungles! It is ideal to know about these time suckers now, with the goal that we can be proactive in keeping away from the things that can ruin our projects.

1. Just crocheting in the front loop

When you are new to crocheting it very well may be anything but difficult to commit this error. Learning where to put your hook in each fastener is VERY significant; it is the premise of this specialty. This slip-up might happen because you did not completely comprehend the manner in which you were instructed to crochet or this is because your hook slips now and again and you aren't prepared enough to see the error immediately.

A powerful method to fix this misstep is to invest some additional energy breaking down each line that you are working. It may feel dull however since you know the brilliant standard of crocheting under the two circles (except if specifically coordinated not to) then you should ensure your lines are worked appropriately until it turns out to be natural.

2. *Your project keeps getting wider and wider*

Everybody makes this misstep at any rate once. I wager you can recall the specific time you began that project and thought, "This will be so natural, it's simply rehashing a similar fastener to and fro!" and after that an hour later you see that your square shape cover is presently a hexagon!

This issue happens when you are not including your connections and you wind up working a greater number of fasteners than required. You could be bending over into one fastener or inadvertently working a connection in the turning chain. The best way to prevent this error from happening is to make those connections!

You could check each column as you finish them, or you can watch out for the state of your work. Try not to burn through significant time working rapidly and afterward understanding that 10 columns back you included an additional connection. Welcome to frog town!

3. *Not counting your rows while you work*

This point and the point above are about not burning through your important time. Much the same as you should tally your fasteners when you are working, you likewise should check the columns. I don't think about you, however I have been working on a task that only required a simple connection rehash and afterward following 20 minutes of careless crocheting I saw that I had quite recently made 5 additional columns!

If you rehash that slip-up different times then you have fundamentally quite recently made and afterward frogged an entire second scarf. The most direct answer for this issue is to utilize a column counter. That could be an extravagant advanced column counter that tallies each line with a basic snap or you can get a fresh start and utilize a pen and scratch pad to make a little tick after each line that you complete.

4. Befuddling US Furthermore, UK Crochet terms

I will be straightforward with you all; when I previously began crocheting I didn't have the foggiest idea about this was a thing. I never ran over this issue until I began composing crochet patterns of my own. I had discharged one of my first patterns to the world and a client from the UK contacted me inquiring as to whether the terms I was utilizing in my pattern were UK or US. With a speedy hunt on the Web, I made sense of what she was alluding to.

For instance, what is known as a solitary crochet (sc) in U.S. terms is known as a twofold crochet (dc) in U.K. terms. (Brain = Blown) With this as a primary concern, it is VERY imperative to check the pattern before you start. If it isn't composed on the pattern, then I do suggest reaching the creator for clarification. On the flipside, if you are a creator, then it is additionally VERY significant that you make it clear to everybody that terms you are utilizing.

5. Using a different weight yarn

The heaviness of the yarn is pivotal when it comes to following a crochet pattern. If you are needing to make a thick scarf from an pattern that requires a #6 yarn yet the sum total of what you have is a #5 then you ought to anticipate the completed thing to seem unique.

Each pattern is composed in view of a specific yarn and even a single switch up or down in weight can shift your result. If you need to go through the yarn that you have nearby, then I propose working your check swatch.

6. Utilizing the wrong hook size

This point and the point above are likewise fundamentally the same errors. Utilizing an inappropriate hook size can drastically change the result of your project. Once more, each pattern is composed considering a specific hook size and changing that will make your connection either excessively tight or excessively loose.

Make a point to read your pattern closely to ensure that you are utilizing the right size. Too, make a point to make your check swatch! You may not understand that you have an inappropriate hook in your grasp and once you see that your size swatch is off, then you have spared yourself a great deal of trouble!

7. Failure to the read the crochet first

When beginning an energizing new project, the exact opposite thing you need to do is invest energy reading each line first. You simply need to get your yarn and your hook and start! After some experience working with crochet designs I do feel that it is a slip-up if you don't read the pattern first. It may not have a colossal effect without fail, however I can recall winding up confounded by an increasingly entangled advance essentially because I didn't read ahead to comprehend the unique circumstance.

Reading the pattern initially can likewise allow you to learn another line early. You don't have to remember each progression yet reading an pattern resembles reading for a test before you take it. It's in every case best to start another crochet project with certainty!

8. Failure to count the starting chain correctly

Wooden crochet hook and blue crochet chain with content that reads 'For Pattern: Double crochet in third chain from the hook and right over. 6 twofold crochets. Start your first DC in chain #6'

The foundation of each crochet project (and likely one of the least pleasant pieces of each project) is that beginning chain. Learning to chain is one of the principal things you will learn when crocheting and it tends to be one of the most befuddling.

A typical misstep when chaining isn't setting your first fastener in the correct chain. This will result in an excessive number of or insufficient fasteners and if you aren't tallying those lines then your task is destined from the beginning. The best way to desist from or fix this issue is to turn out to be contented with how to chain and how to tally the chains.

9. Not creating a gauge swatch/not working the gauge swatch when following a pattern

The check swatch is something that ought to be learned at an opportune time. This basic square can spare you heaps of time and exertion when following an pattern and can make your own structures a lot simpler to pursue. The check will decide the strain expected to make the pattern accurately.

I for one crochet more on the tight side so if I start following an pattern composed by somebody who has a looser strain then my last task will be excessively small. What an exercise in futility! Make a point to make those measure swatches (and incorporate them in your very own structures) and if you find that your pressure is different than invest a touch of energy changing by expanding or diminishing your hook size, for instance.

10. Keeping Your Project Straight

Often times, keeping your project straight when you're working a level piece is probably the hardest piece of crocheting when you're first beginning. Presently, your project probably won't be this radically skewed, yet now and again your piece that should have straight edges, will start looking bended. This issue has an extremely basic arrangement!

If your project starts bending in all over, this is in all probability brought about by you inadvertently including connections where they should not be. This could be by unintentionally including two connections in one of the lines in the column when you need not bother with an expansion, which will change the state of the line.

Or on the other hand, frequently, it is because the last connection of the column is worked in an inappropriate line. When you arrive at the finish of the column, you need to ensure that you crochet your last fastener in the highest point of the principal connection from the past line. You would prefer not to place a connection in the chains that began that round. If you set the last connection there, it includes one more line than you need, which then makes your level piece start bending.

If it's difficult to determine what the highest point of the last line in the line is, focus on the two circles over the fasten resemble. Monitor these. The chains will have a strand and one circle framing them, rather than the ordinary post that a crochet connection has, and the two circles at the top that you put your hook through. For whatever length of time that you monitor where the fastens are at, your project will remain straight the entire time!

Not understanding tension

As you accomplish an ever-increasing number of patterns, you'll start seeing the word strain being tossed around. I don't get it's meaning in reference to crochet however? Strain alludes to how tight your lines are. If you have a tight pressure then your material you are making with your yarn will be tight with scarcely any transparency in the connection. If you have a slight pressure, then your lines will be open and loose. The objective is to have same pressure all through your project, with the goal that your connection snugness never changes as you make your task.

You probably won't pull the yarn more tightly by any stretch of the imagination, and you'll wind up with greater lines. To abstain from going one way or the other, you'll need to ensure that while you are crocheting your fasteners that you pull on the connection enough to ensure it is loose, however not enough to make it overly tight. I tell the best way to do this in the video for this post.

11. Failure to leave enough tail of yarn

Weaving in the closures is most likely everybody's least most loved piece of crocheting. No, shockingly you can't simply cut the yarn and expect no one will notice - and after that battling because your strand is too short.

There is no difference between stopping a task, including another bundle of yarn, or alternating between different shades of yarn; you have to ensure that you leave a sound length to weave in. I propose leaving in any event 5-6 inches of yarn with the goal that this process can be as effortless as possible.

Chapter 8   Tips And Tricks To Crocheting

Every crocheter requires tips and tricks to become a pro. These tips and tricks help make things easier when you begin crocheting.

Crocheting Using Thread

When it comes to crocheting thread, remember that smaller is bigger. Threads are labeled according to their thickness. The thicker the thread, the smaller is the number. It is counterintuitive, but the more you crochet, the more you will get used to it.

1. As a beginner, you can always start with a crochet thread three, then move up to a five and ten. Size twenty or thirty threads can be used once you have built up your skills.

2. As with the crochet threads, follow the same approach with steel crochet hooks. The smaller the size, the bigger the crochet hook. You can also look at the mm size that is usually printed on the hook itself. For example, a hook sized nine is 1.25 mm while the hook sized ten is 1.15 mm.

3. As a beginner, you should start with a hook size that the pattern calls for. Once you have honed your skills a little more, you can adjust your hooks based on your comfort level and gauge.

4. For beginners, it is always good to use steel crochet hooks. These hooks are much easier to use when it comes to working with thread.

5. People often find crocheting using thread more difficult compared to using yarn, and it is only because of the thinner hooks involved. When you are working with the thread, all you need to do is choose a hook that has a bigger handle - that's all!

6. When purchasing thread, always buy a crochet thread and steer clear from embroidery or sewing thread. Although you can crochet with almost anything that resembles yarn or thread, you can make your life easier by sticking to the kind of thread that is meant for crocheting.

7. When you work with yarn overs, make sure to work closely with the crochet hook head. You always want to ensure that the work on the hook is done above the section of the hook where it starts to get wider. Otherwise, your loops will be extremely loose.

8. Another tip would be to thread around your non-crocheting hand, so it is easier to control your tension. This is extremely helpful when thread crocheting.

Crocheting Hacks with Yarn

1. To prevent the balls of yarn from rolling away while you are crocheting, put them in a hand wipe container. Just make sure to wash and clean it first. The yarn can be pulled through the hole of the hand wipe container.

2. Use bobby pins or safety pins, or even a paper clip to mark your rows, or stitch a colored yarn or thread into the valley of the first stitch. Bobby pins and paper clips can be pulled out later once you are done.

3. Use pencil boxes or jewelry boxes, or even a toothbrush holder to store your hooks. Food containers and snack containers can also do the trick.

4. Using Excel sheets to map out your patterns. This is a great way to keep track of where you left off when your crocheting gets interrupted. You can also make the pattern larger to decrease eyestrain.

5. To figure out the amount of yarn or thread needed for a certain project, calculate the number of rows you can get out of one skein/ball, and then determine how many rows your project requires. Then, divide the number of rows the project requires the number of rows your ball gives you. You will be able to calculate how much yarn is needed this way.

6. If you are worried about purchasing too much-colored yarn that you won't be using in the future, just buy white washable yarn and dye it according to the pattern's colors.

7. To keep your project in place, use yarn needles instead of hooks to weave the ends back through. This holds the project better and eliminates the chances of the yarn traveling.

8. Instead of ironing your projects, which is not always ideal, mix water and starch in equal parts and spray liberally on your project. Leave to dry on a flat surface.

9. To store patterns in a three-ring notebook, use sheet protectors.

10. Keeping an index card with the lists of hooks and yarns you have is a great way to keep inventory. This ensures that the next time you are short of crochet supplies, you already know what you need.

11. Yarns and other unfinished projects can be kept in zipper bags.

12. It is always a good idea to keep foldable sewing scissors so that they don't snag in your crocheting bag.

13. When in doubt, sew more tightly with string than you would with yarn. Try not to stitch so firmly that you hurt your hands. Knit somewhat more firmly than normal (except if you're now a skilled crocheter, at that point, simply do what you generally do!).

14. Pay attention to the steps you're about to follow before you figure with thread crochet. Jumping from an okay hook size, labored with a cumbersome yarn all the way down to thread crochet can make your thread paintings appear unbearably tiny. Steadily work your way down to the smaller sizes.

15. Always do your crochet work in a good light so that you don't strain your eyes. This also makes crocheting easier. This is the same reason why, as beginners, you need to work with a lighter colored thread as it makes it easier for you to find those little stitches.

16. Crocheting is fun! Sure, it does have its own challenges, but that's only something you'll need to overcome at the beginning. Learning takes time, so be patient with yourself and enjoy each project you work on.

17. Always choose beginner patterns when you're starting off. This will make it easier for you to learn how to combine stitches and learn the ropes of crocheting.

18. Working with a simple crochet swatch that uses basic stitches is always ideal, simply to get the best results, minus the pressure of going through with a pattern.

Starting and finishing project

Starting project

Before making any stitches, it's important to understand how to hold a crochet hook. Part of this is determined by handedness; left-handed individuals don't have to learn to crochet in the typical manner (i.e., holding the hook in the right hand), but they should keep in mind that most patterns are written for right-handed crocheters. This may make it worthwhile to learn to crochet with the right hand, but directions can be reversed with practice, so left-handers are under no duress to use their non-dominant hand. Because the majority of individuals are right-handed, this work focuses on learning to crochet with the right hand.

Ways to hold a crochet hook are numerous, but the two most common are referred to as the knife hold and the pencil hold. Neither is better than the other is, only different. New crocheters are encouraged to try both holds to find the one that is the most comfortable for them.

With the knife hold, the hand faces downward with the hook under the palm, much the way one would hold a knife. The pencil hold is the opposite: The palm faces upward with the hook grasped between the thumb and two forefingers, like holding a pencil.

Finishing project

Properly finishing a crocheted piece is important for several reasons. First, the finishing process will settle the stitches, giving the piece a professional look. Second, finishing allows the crocheter to form the piece into the correct shape and straighten any shaping issues. Third, finishing items properly makes seaming and adding embellishments easier. Any way you look at it, then, finishing is a necessary part of the crocheting process.

The two main steps in finishing are weaving in the yarn ends and blocking. While many crafters don't see either process as particularly 'fun', learning to perform them properly does take some of the anxiety out of the work. Hopefully, after finishing a few projects, blocking and weaving in ends will start to feel like just one more step in a crochet project.

Chapter 9   Crochet Goal

Crochet fans are looking forward to finishing crochet creations, which are usually useful, desirable, or helpful items in a certain way. Popular designs involve Afghans, crocheted blankets, baby booties, scarves, caps, and squares of granny, shawls, belts, tote bags, and many others. A range of different items can be crocheted, from hats, shoes, and curtains.

It is also necessary to use different components in other products. Crochet trims as well as edgings, for instance, are common projects; you may attach these to crocheted products, knitted items, including sewn pieces (including ready-made supermarket-bought items), such as purchasing some shoes, towels, and pillowcases, and applying a crocheted finish to the whole.

Techniques for crochet are also common activities.

Not many crocheters are obsessed with crochet tasks being done. In addition to the tasks, there are many other objectives, objectives, and incentives of crochet.

The Crochet Base Unit: A Crochet Sew Every crochet design comprises of crochet stitches. The following are the fundamental crochet stitches:

Crochet Stitch Patterns

To create unique stitch designs, crochet fans may adapt the simple stitches in unique ways. Multiple different looks can be created; lacy or flat, decorative or translucent, patterned, or simple stitch designs can be used. Many common patterns of crochet stitches are about as follows: • Shell stitch

• V stitch

- Cluster stitch

Crochet Patterns

A crochet trend is a collection of crocheting guidance for an item, or a connected set of materials at times.

Where to Find Crochet Patterns

There are many locations where you can locate crochet designs. There are plenty of trends available on the web for download.

There are also several crochet designs available on the market.

There are crochet publications as this, as well as art magazines and articles of overall interest that crochet designs also are contained.

How to Read a Crochet Pattern

Crochet designs typically use acronyms to write their designs to save paper. You need to comprehend that and reacquaint yourself with that of the acronyms included within the pattern to understand a crochet model.

Typically, in a sensible place, you will be able to locate the acronyms. We put the acronyms near the top within each pattern before the instructions with the patterns we posted on our website.

If the template was from a publication or journal, you can typically find the acronyms mentioned at the front or rear of the paper elsewhere.

Similarities and Differences between Crochet and Knitting

There is often ambiguity about crochet and knitting. The methods share some common aspects; for example, wool is used by both crocheters as well as knitters to construct each design.

Different sorts of designs can be made using either method: afghans, shawls, caps, scarves, etc. You could tell at a glance how well an individual is knitting or crocheting from looking at the materials they are using.

When (s)he uses a pin, (s)he crochets; when she uses two pointing needles, or maybe a wounded knitting stitch, (s)he knits.

Who Can Crochet? Could You? Is Crochet the Right Hobby for You?

If you have never crocheted since, you may shudder to think if it's a meaningful leisure activity, or whether it's something you'd want to get engaged with. Will crocheting require particular talent?

The good news: you can crochet, just about anybody's thing is crocheting. There have been young kids crocheting, as well as incredibly old men. Both the crocheting of males and females. Folks from around the globe crochet.

Disabled people are crocheting, and even blinded people are engaged. Poor people are crocheting, and so are the rich.

To crocheting, there are almost no disincentives, but you may want to be conscious of a few imperatives before you begin.,

Crochet Tension

What is crochet tension? In crocheting, tension is how tight the stitches are. It is also known as a gauge. Gauge is the number of stitches and rows per inch that are brought about by working with a specific yarn and hook size. How tight or lose your stitches are, is determined by how you hold your yarn, the type of hook you are using, and the thickness of your yarn.

When you purchase yarn, the yarn label recommends the hook size to use and the gauge to achieve with that specific yarn. Tension affects the density, size, hang, and thickness of your crochet. It can also be affected by your posture or mood. It is important to get your crochet tension right always. So, how is crochet tension determined by how you hold your yarn?

Many beginners of crocheting hold the yarn too tightly. It makes the stitches hard, and crocheting the next row becomes even harder. It will also affect the end product of our crochet as it will be smaller than the size expected.

Why is it so important to get the right tension on your yarn? Knowing the best tension to apply is important as it reflects on the results of your crochet. When crocheting, your yarn should flow smoothly through your fingers without inconsistencies. You should not strain it or let it hang loosely.

It is also important to know that we all crochet differently, and no crochets are the same. Some are tighter than others. The most crucial thing in crocheting is your comfort in holding the yarn and hook. If the way you hold your yarn affects the gauge, we can change that with a few instructions. The best way to perfect your gauge is through practice, but there are different ways to reduce tension in your crochets.

Train Yourself to Pull the Yarn from the Center of the Skein

Every skein has an open end on the inside and outside. Many crocheters have confirmed that using the yarn from the outside causes the skein to keep bounce all over, affecting your tension. When you pull your yarn from the center, it slides smoothly through your fingers. In some skeins, it is not easy to find the open end in the center; we should, therefore, be careful when doing it.

Wind the Skein into a Ball

It might take your time, but it reduces tension in your crochets. When you do this, you can get your yarn from any end you choose. You can also buy a ball winder, and it will help you combine two colors to one skein.

Yarn Bowl

Yarn bowls hold your yarn in place and keep it from tangling and falling into the arms of your children or pet, especially cats. A yarn bowl will save you a lot of trouble from the yarn bouncing all over the place, increasing tension to the yarn tangling.

Tension Regulator

It is easy to make and inexpensive. It is the best solution to regulating the tension. We wear a tension regulator on the base of the index finger, and you pass your yarn over its stitches. It regulates the tension on the yarn easily as it glides smoothly over the stitches.

Yarn Type

Tension can be a result of the type of yarn you are using. Some yarns like Lily Sugar 'N Cream are not beginner-friendly. I did not say it is not a great yarn, but for inexperienced crocheters, they should work with stretchy yarns. Some yarns are not suitable for crocheters, still figuring out their tension. Hard and tough yarns also make it difficult for a beginner to count the stitches.

Hook Size

To know whether to use a large or small hook size, you should look at your first row and foundation chain. If both of them are loose, you should change to a smaller hook, and if they are tight, then a bigger one would be good to go. You should play up and down your hook size to get the correct tension.

Are You a Tight or Loose Crocheter?

As I mentioned earlier, we all crochet differently, and it is acceptable. If you are a loose crocheter, you should change your hook to a smaller one than recommended, and if you are a tight crocheter, you should get a larger hook.

Chapter 10   Holding the Yarn

Just as we mentioned in holding the hook, there is also no right or wrong way to hold the yarn. The best way is the one that offers comfort and smooth crocheting. We usually hold the yarn in the non-dominant hand. This hand feeds the yarn to the hook in crocheting. The non-dominant hand also eases or increases the tension on the yarn to determine how loose or tight your patterns will be.

When you are training to crochet, it is not easy to figure out how to hold the yarn. The good news is that it doesn't have to be easy. We have a basic way to hold the yarn that can be personalized to fit in your crocheting. Let us go through the steps on how to hold the yarn.

1. You should hold the hook in your dominant hand. Grip the hook with a knife grip or pencil grip, whichever gives you comfort. It helps you know the importance of yarn hold.

2. Use your other hand to hold the yarn. If the right hand is dominant, use the left one, and if your left hand is the dominant one, use the right one. Either of the holds will be the same, not considering the hand that will hold the yarn.

3. Spread your fingers and flatten your hand. By spreading your fingers, you will feed the yarn between them easily. Some people curve their fingers after the yarn is placed between the fingers, as they feel comfortable that way.

4. You hold the beginning of the yarn with your thumb and index finger. In this next step, there are two ways of doing it. In the first method, some people hold the thread between their ring and pinkie from under the palm.

In the second method, some people prefer holding the thread between their ring and middle finger. Either way is correct; what matters is your comfort.

5. Keep pulling the yarn to bring it diagonally on top of your hand. Some people pull at least 15cm that goes past their index finger while others prefer working with the yarn close to their hand.

6. To ease tension on your fingers, you should spread them and close them to increase. Spreading and closing the fingers helps you to tighten and loosen your hold on the yarn. This movement of fingers is a cause of the type of pattern you are crocheting.

7. To have control over the yarn, you should hold it with your thumb and index finger. Press it between the two fingers to increase or reduce the tension. Some people allow the yarn to dangle freely instead of pressing it between the thumb and index finger.

8. For security purposes, you should wrap the yarn on your pinkie finger. You should wrap it from below your arm and hold it between your ring and pinkie finger. You should then direct the yarn on top of your pinkie then move it back between your ring finger and pinkie for a good hold on the yarn. By doing this, you will get more tension and hold the yarn securely.

9. After the basic hold on the yarn, you should wrap it around your index finger. It should not be done tightly but should be comfortable around your finger to avoid discomfort.

How Do You Find the Right Yarn Hold for Your Crochet?

We have read many health issues brought about by the way we hold our yarn. People have developed problems like carpal tunnel syndrome, tendonitis, or arthritis in the past caused by how they hold their hook with their dominant hand. However, we should also pay attention to the non-dominant hand that holds the yarn.

As we mentioned earlier, it is important in regulating tension and providing a smooth crocheting motion. In crocheting, we should discover the method of holding the yarn that is suitable for each one of us.

Any method you choose to hold your yarn is correct only if it is effective in regulating the tension of the yarn and giving you comfort in the movement of your hands. Most people who crochet discover that their comfortable way of holding the yarn causes cramping or pain if they crochet for long periods. Some find that they need more physical effort when working with some stitch patterns.

To some people, comfort in holding the yarn reduces their speed, and others form uneven spaced and sized stitches. Many people think that these problems are effects of the way they hold their hook, and some try adjusting it with no tangible results. Many others change their hook types with no visible effect. The truth, however, is these problems are because of the way they hold and move their yarn.

Did that surprise you? Well, I didn't expect that either. The correct tension for good stitching requires a smooth movement of the yarn when the hook pulls it. If there is a big space between the yarn-guiding finger and the hook, the end stitches become loose on some parts. In such cases, the fingers hold tightly and might get some injuries, or you must keep adjusting the yarn through the fingers. It slows the work, injures the fingers, and causes uneven patterns on the fabric.

On the other hand, some people tighten the yarn around their palm or finger, causing difficulties in moving the yarn. The hook fights the resistance pulling the non-dominant hand with the force. It forces them to keep adjusting and wrapping the yarn again. The two methods above might result in a poor quality of the finished work, stress injuries, reduced speed in working, and messing the crochet rhythm.

Nonetheless, if we develop a system that can give two partial tension points, we would not need many muscles to regulate the movement of the yarn. If in crocheting, we can have a system that works like the sewing machine, we can reduce the different health issues caused by the way we hold our yarn. So, how can we develop such a system?

We can develop that through experiments and a lot of observation. We all have different shapes of the hands, such as narrow or wider palms, shorter or longer fingers. Some of us have flexible hands than others, while others have sweaty hands than others.

All these unique features in our hands affect how we hold our yarn in one way or another. For instance, a person with arthritis will need a lot of effort to hold the yarn between the fingers, whereas a person whose fingers find it easy to hold may find it easy to hold the yarn between the fingers. Likewise, hands that sweat provide more friction than hands that do not sweat. The dry hands can be injured easily than the sweaty hands.

When you've held your yarn properly, and it is gently passing through your fingers, you apply tension in two places. By doing that, you can keep a good distance from the hook to work on the yarn. This distance should be short to be able to make even stitches.

If you are using the index finger to guide the yarn, the distance between the hook and the guiding finger should not be more than an inch. In threadwork where the stitches should be tight, the distance should be less than that. The looseness of a stitch is as a result of the amount of yarn in the mentioned distance.

Therefore, you should start by making sure that your hands are straight and the palm should face you. If you have space between your fingers, then you should wrap the yarn around your pinky finger once instead of holding it with your fist. If there are no spaces between your fingers, then you should increase tension by entwining the yarn between your fingers.

The next thing to observe should be your skin texture. Are your hands dry or moist? If they are moist, they will increase tension naturally and, therefore, few wrappings. If they are dry, you will wrap halfway on the pinky as yarn flows fast on dry hands. It will be easy to keep and

How is the flexibility of your hands? Is it hard for you to bend your palm for the thumb and pinky to touch each other? If yes, you will have to guide the yarn using your middle finger. If it is easy for your thumb and pinky to touch, then you have a flexible hand; it will be easy to keep a good working distance.

It is also good to change your style of holding the yarn to test its effectiveness. A change may be uncomfortable at first, but you should work through it to check if it will be painless. You never know, maybe a change is an answer to unswerving stitches with a painless procedure.

You are correctly holding the yarn while stitching, but are you looking out for the roll of yarn on the other end to keep it from tangling?

Tangling of the yarn is an issue that disturbs even the most experienced people in this field. Working with several skeins of yarn can frustrate you as a yarn can tangle with itself or with the other colors. Tangling of the yarn waste a lot of time, and you might find yourself taking time to make some simple patterns than necessary. Let us look at some tips to keep your yarn from tangling as you are crocheting.

Roll Your Skeins into Balls of Yarn

Our skeins packaging is not easy to work maneuver. It is packed loosely and makes the skeins to tangle. Repackaging your skeins in a tight ball shape, this will ensure no tangling of the skein.

How Do You Pull Your Yarn?

I know we said earlier that there is no right way and wrong way to do it, but most crocheters agree that pulling your yarn from the center makes it tangle. The most advisable way to do it is to find the end of your yarn inside and pull from there. This way, the yarn slides without tangling out of the skein.

Container Use

In crocheting, you can't do away with creativity. Some crocheters have found it easy to crochet with their skeins inside a container. You should get a container and put your skein in it. Drill a hole where you will pull your yarn through. This method is effective as you keep your yarn away from the environment. It is advisable to get a clear container to keep you from checking the yarn size. If you are using more than one color, you can get more than one container.

Conclusion

Crochet beginners and experts alike enjoy creating projects from patterns. Although it is possible to use the beginner stitches and make a blanket without a pattern, a pattern will provide more detail. Some patterns use small crochet appliques or alternating patterns and the project patterns show how to do it.

Many crocheters learn to make their own patterns and graphs from the abbreviations and symbols they have learned. Once you master all of the stitches, you will be able to make your own patterns so others can make project you have designed.

Using patterns may seem difficult and overwhelming at first but once you are used to seeing the abbreviations and symbols your skills will improve. Stick to patterns and graphs for beginners, these use beginner stitches so you can learn at your own pace.

Learning the skill to read and follow graphs and patterns will allow you to create more than just a scarf or simple throw. You will be able to complete heirloom quality projects, winter clothing such as sweaters, mittens, gloves, hats and scarfs, dresses, home décor such as doilies or place mats and runners, and even toys for the kids.

It is also necessary to use different components in other products. Crochet trims as well as edgings, for instance, are common projects; you may attach these to crocheted products, knitted items, including sewn pieces (including ready-made supermarket-bought items), such as purchasing some shoes, towels, and pillow cases, and applying a crocheted finish to the whole.

It is only by practicing that you will become perfect. Moving to advanced crocheting levels requires that you practice for a long time. Use cheap yarns to practice and sharpen your crocheting skills. When practicing, you will be able to identify your areas of weaknesses and improve on them. I prefer that you can start learning with slipknots, then move to work with stitches into the chain, then turning chains and then finally have a thorough look at the anatomy of a stitch observing both the front loop and back loop.

For a beginner, it is advised that you avoid expensive yarns. Inexpensive yarns should be your friend. You should also avoid slippery yarns as well as anything with texture. As a beginner, textured yarns will make everything to be hard because it will be difficult for you to see your stitches. You are likely to be frustrated when you are not able to see your stitches. It is therefore recommended that you use smooth acrylic yarn that has a medium weight. Again, it is only by practicing that you will become perfect in this field. Crocheting is an enjoyable hobby, and I hope you will always have the desire to crochet during your free time.

Generally, you also have to learn about ethics and yarn. This means that you have taken a considerable amount of your time to understand how you can make sustainable yarn choices that will touch on things like vegan yarn and organic yarn. There are also other yarn decisions that will relate to your personal ethics and beliefs around the society, the environment, and animals around. For instance, my personal ethics will not allow me to crochet something like a thong because my perception of it concerning the society around me is negative or rather considered immoral. Therefore, before doing some projects, you have to put some considerations as well.

The best way for you to find it easy learning how to crochet is by having to make a good hook choice. However, the challenge that most beginners do encounter comes when choosing the right hook. Every person has his/her preferences and therefore, what may seem suitable for one person may not be suitable for another person. Furthermore, different projects and different yarns will require hooks of different styles, sizes, and shapes. Don't be scared by this. After doing your first few projects, you will be able to identify the best hook that fits you.

Understanding the anatomy of the hook will help you made the right decisions when choosing hooks for different projects.

Our hand posture plays a big role in crocheting. Sometimes ignoring the crochet basics can be the cause of our hand and wrist pains. Our bodies are always communicating with us if only we could listen. If you strain any part of the body, you will experience some discomfort. When crocheting, to avoid the pains mentioned above, how should we position our hand? Some people are fond of flexing their wrists even when crocheting, but it is advisable always to keep them straight. You should make this a habit even if you are not crocheting. It might be hard at the beginning, but a wrist brace should come in hand and align the wrist.

We've come to the end. Thank you very much for choosing this book. I hope you found it helpful in your journey of discovery of crochet and in the creation of your first works.

Sarah Boulard

Made in the USA
Columbia, SC
03 June 2020